WHO DO YOU SAY THAT I AM?

The Pro Ecclesia Series

Books in The Pro Ecclesia Series are "for the Church." The series is sponsored by the Center for Catholic and Evangelical Theology, founded by Carl Braaten and Robert Jenson in 1991. The series seeks to nourish the Church's faithfulness to the gospel of Jesus Christ through a theology that is self-critically committed to the biblical, dogmatic, liturgical, and ethical traditions that form the foundation for a fruitful ecumenical theology. The series reflects a commitment to the classical tradition of the Church as providing the resources critically needed by the various churches as they face modern and post-modern challenges. The series will include books by individuals as well as collections of essays by individuals and groups. The Editorial Board will be drawn from various Christian traditions.

OTHER TITLES IN THE SERIES:

The Morally Divided Body, edited by Michael Root and James J. Buckley

Christian Theology and Islam, edited by Michael Root and James J. Buckley

Who Do You Say that I Am?

Proclaiming and Following Jesus Today

edited by
Michael Root &
James J. Buckley

CASCADE *Books* • Eugene, Oregon

WHO DO YOU SAY THAT I AM?
Proclaiming and Following Jesus Today

The Pro Ecclesia Series 3

Copyright © 2014 Wipf and Stock Publishers. All rights reserved. Except for brief quotations in critical publications or reviews, no part of this book may be reproduced in any manner without prior written permission from the publisher. Write: Permissions, Wipf and Stock Publishers, 199 W. 8th Ave., Suite 3, Eugene, OR 97401.

Cascade Books
An Imprint of Wipf and Stock Publishers
199 W. 8th Ave., Suite 3
Eugene, OR 97401

www.wipfandstock.com

ISBN 13: 978-1-62032-586-5

Cataloging-in-Publication data:

Who do you say that I am? : proclaiming and following Jesus today / edited by Michael Root and James J. Buckley

x + 108 p.; 23 cm—Includes bibliographical references and index.

The Pro Ecclesia Series 3

ISBN 13: 978-1-62032-586-5

1. Jesus Christ—Person and offices. 2. Christian life. 3. Christianity and culture. 4. I. Root, Michael, 1951–. II. Buckley, James J. III. Title. IV. Series.

BT203 .W480 2014

Manufactured in the USA.

Contents

Contributors · vii

Preface · ix
MICHAEL ROOT AND JAMES J. BUCKLEY

1 The Search for the Real Jesus · 1
CARL E. BRAATEN

2 Jesus and the Historians · 21
DALE C. ALLISON, JR.

3 Why the Roman Cross? · 39
KATHERINE SONDEREGGER

4 The Benedictine Jesus · 52
JOSEPH BOTTUM

5 "Lord, to Whom Shall We Go?
You Have the Words of Eternal Life":
Jesus as Lord in Prayer and Pastoral Care · 63
KATHRYN GREENE-MCCREIGHT

6 Proclaiming the Lord Jesus Christ · 75
FLEMING RUTLEDGE

7 Behold the Lamb of God Who Does *What*?
Gossiping about Jesus and Giving Our Neighbors
the (Boney) Finger · 88
DANIEL M. BELL, JR.

Contributors

Dale C. Allison, Jr., is the Richard J. Dearborn Professor of New Testament at Princeton Theological Seminary. He is the author of numerous books, including *Resurrecting Jesus: The Earliest Christian Tradition and Its Interpreters* (2005), *The Luminous Dusk* (2006), *The Historical Christ and the Theological Jesus* (2009), *Constructing Jesus: Memory, Imagination, and History* (2010), and *A Critical and Exegetical Commentary on the Epistle of James* (2013).

Daniel M. Bell, Jr., is Professor of Theological Ethics at Lutheran Theological Southern Seminary and an Elder in The United Methodist Church. He is author of *Liberation Theology after the End of History* (2001), *Just War as Christian Discipleship* (2009), and *The Economy of Desire* (2012).

Joseph Bottum is one of the nation's most widely published essayists and poets, with work appearing in magazines and newspapers from *The Atlantic* to *The Wall Street Journal*. A bestselling e-book author, Bottum is the former editor in chief of the journal *First Things* and former literary editor of *The Weekly Standard*. He holds a PhD in philosophy, lectures widely on literary and religious topics, and lives with his family far off in the Black Hills of South Dakota. His latest work is *An Anxious Age: The Post-Protestant Ethic and the Spirit of America* (2015).

Carl E. Braaten is professor emeritus of systematic theology of the Lutheran School of Theology at Chicago. With his wife, LaVonne, and Robert and Blanche Jenson, he cofounded the Center for Catholic and Evangelical Theology. With Robert Jenson he was the coeditor of *Pro Ecclesia: A Journal of Catholic and Evangelical Theology*. He resides with his wife in Sun City West, Arizona.

Contributors

James J. Buckley is Professor of Theology at Loyola University Maryland. He is a member of the North American Lutheran Catholic dialogue and an associate director of the Center for Catholic and Evangelical Theology. He contributed to and edited *The Blackwell Companion to Catholicism* (2008) and *The Morally Divided Body* (Cascade Books, 2012).

Kathryn Greene-McCreight is a Priest Associate at The Episcopal Church at Yale and a theological writer.

Michael Root is Professor of Systematic Theology at The Catholic University of America and Executive Director of the Center for Catholic and Evangelical Theology. He was formerly the Director of the Institute for Ecumenical Research, Strasbourg, France.

Fleming Rutledge is a preacher and teacher known throughout the mainline Protestant denominations of the United States, Canada, and parts of the United Kingdom. One of the first women to be ordained to the priesthood of the Episcopal Church, she served in parish ministry for twenty-two years. Fourteen of those years were spent at Grace Church on Lower Broadway at Tenth Street, New York City. Her most recent position was as guest lecturer in preaching at the University of Toronto School of Theology. She is the author of seven books, the most recent being *And God Spoke to Abraham* (2011). She has received a grant from the Louisville Institute to complete a two-volume work about the meaning of the crucifixion. Her Web site is www.generousorthodoxy.org.

Katherine Sonderegger is a priest of the Episcopal Church. She has been Professor of Theology at Virginia Theological Seminary since 2002. Prior to her appointment at Virginia, she served as Professor of Religion at Middlebury College in Vermont. She is the author of *That Jesus Christ Was Born a Jew: Karl Barth's Doctrine of Israel* (1992). Her research interests lie in the areas of doctrinal theology, as well as the dogmatic theology of Karl Barth.

Preface

Michael Root and James J. Buckley

No question is more central to Christian living and preaching and theology than Jesus' question to his disciples: Who do you say that I am? The Center for Catholic and Evangelical Theology has been sponsoring conferences on various questions for many years. But none is more basic than this question we posed for our 2011 meeting. Some would have it that pastors and theologians, biblical exegetes and historians, dogmatic and moral theologians Catholic and Evangelical have more differences than similarities in the way Christians with such diverse vocations respond to Jesus' question. And there is little doubt that there sometimes seem to be unbridgeable gulfs between the way historians and believers, Internet gossipers and preachers, classical christological debates and present-day praying and pastoral care implicitly or explicitly address the Lord's question. But the authors here address these and other issues in ways we find remarkably convergent, as if a "Catholic and Evangelical theology" for proclaiming and following Jesus today has emerged, or is indeed emerging.

This is not to say that there are no important differences among these authors. We invite readers to seek the differences that emerge as each author responds to the book's question. How can the often inane gossip about Jesus that pervades the land (as Daniel Bell points out) relate to seriously joyful matters of Christian discipleship? How does the work of historians relate to the quest for the real Jesus (Carl Braaten)—or how does Jesus' expectation of an imminent end speak directly to our own apocalyptic times (Dale Allison)? What is the significance of Jesus' death on a Roman cross (as Kathryn Sonderegger asks) for Christians in a world of persistent violence? How does Jesus Christ transform our pastoral care (Kathryn Greene-McCreight) and preaching (Fleming Rutledge)? What shall we (like Jody Bottum) make

Preface

of the first pope to write books on Jesus that aspire to hold together the historical, the spiritual, and the theological? We invite readers to seek out the differences in these essays, even as they remember their common ground in aspiring to a genuine Catholic and Evangelical theology.

Michael Root, Catholic University of America
James J. Buckley, Loyola University Maryland
July 2012

1

The Search for the Real Jesus

Carl E. Braaten

Introduction

MANY YEARS AGO I walked into the office of Paul Tillich at Harvard University to ask about a dissertation topic. With hardly a moment's hesitation Tillich said, "You must write on Martin Kähler. But first you must translate his famous book, *Der sogenannte historische Jesus und der geschichtliche, biblische Christus.*"[1] Who in the world was Martin Kähler? But you don't argue with your doctor father. I went to the Harvard library and checked out many of Kähler's books, including the one Tillich assigned to me. Soon I figured out why Tillich wanted me to translate Kähler's book into English. Tillich had just published the second volume of his *Systematic Theology*. In it he made this statement: "The attempt of historical criticism to find the empirical truth about Jesus of Nazareth was a failure. The historical Jesus, namely, the Jesus behind the symbols of his reception as the Christ, not only did not appear but receded farther and farther with every new step.... The result of the new (and very old) questioning is not a picture of the so-called historical Jesus but the insight that there is no picture behind the biblical one which could be made scientifically probable."[2]

---

1. Martin Kähler, *The So-Called Historical Jesus and the Historic, Biblical Christ*, trans. and ed. Carl E. Braaten (Philadelphia: Fortress, 1964).

2. Paul J. Tillich, *Systematic Theology* (Chicago: University of Chicago Press, 1957) 2:102.

Who Do You Say That I Am?

Kähler was Tillich's professor of dogmatics at the University of Halle. In using the phrase "the so-called historical Jesus," Tillich was obviously echoing the basic thesis of Kähler's book, namely, that the search for Jesus behind the Gospels results in a "so-called historical Jesus," the Jesus of critical historiography. The title of Kähler's book contrasts "the so-called historical Jesus" with the "historic, biblical Christ" portrayed by the four canonical Gospels. The Gospels are written testimonies given by followers of Jesus who believed in him as the Christ, the risen Lord, and the Son of God. The scientific attempt to shake out the facts from the faith-filled memories of Jesus as the Christ will never get us any closer to the real Jesus. The real Jesus is the "historic, biblical Christ."

A lot of gossip was reporting Tillich to have said, "If historical critics today were to prove that Jesus never existed, it would not make any difference to Christian faith." I have never found where Tillich said that, but if he did he was possibly reiterating Kähler's assertion that the faith of believers in Christ is not dependent on what scholars prove about the historical Jesus, positively or negatively. When Tillich was a theological student, Arthur Drews published his book *The Christ Myth*.[3] He used the methods of historical science to prove that Jesus never existed. The book created a storm of protests in Germany but found echoes of support in England, France, and Holland. Once the fate of the historical figure of Jesus is placed in the hands of historical science, theology cannot control the results. Kähler—and Tillich after him—said that Christian faith is based on the apostolic testimonies to Jesus the Christ, not on the latest findings of historical scientists.

My Harvard dissertation argued that Kähler's judgment was valid not only with reference to the original quest of the historical Jesus, but from a theological point of view it is perennially valid, and therefore equally applicable in relation to what has been called the "new quest" of the Bultmannians as well as the current quests now being conducted by scholars of every stripe, from the neoliberals of the "Jesus Seminar" to those more conservative like N. T. Wright.

---

3. Arthur Drews, *The Christ Myth*, trans. C. Deslisle Burns, Westminster College-Oxford Classics in the Study of Religion (1910, reprint Amherst, NY: Prometheus, 1998).

I. The Kähler Renaissance

When I went to the University of Heidelberg to do what Tillich told me to do, I discovered to my great delight that a Kähler renaissance was underway. Kähler's book had been written more than a decade before Albert Schweitzer's *The Quest of the Historical Jesus*,[4] but it was Schweitzer's that shook the theological world. Most historians and theologians accepted Schweitzer's judgment that the nineteenth-century attempts to write a "life of Jesus" were failures. Whether written from a conservative, liberal, or mediating position, the biographers tended to find a Jesus they were looking for. They depicted the figure of Jesus after their own image. They put their own ideas into the mouth of Jesus. They succumbed to what Henry Cadbury called "the peril of modernizing Jesus."[5]

After the Second World War theologians in Germany rediscovered the relevance of Kähler for their own constructive work. Rudolf Bultmann was the dominant New Testament theologian in the 1950s and 1960s. The doubts that Schweitzer raised about the possibility of writing a biography of Jesus were increased by Bultmann to the highest possible pitch, when he said: "I think we can now know almost nothing concerning the life and personality of Jesus."[6] Bultmann also accepted Kähler's claim that Christian faith is not based on the figure of the historical Jesus as reconstructed by critical historiography.

Karl Barth, Emil Brunner,[7] and Paul Tillich, contemporaries of Bultmann, also concurred with Kähler. In the 1930s they were called dialectical theologians, but in the course of time each went his own way. Time will permit me to offer only a sample of Barth's insights, which both Brunner and Tillich shared.

Barth contributed to the Kähler renaissance. In his *Church Dogmatics* he wrote, "It is an abiding merit of Martin Kähler, which cannot be overpraised, that in his work *Der sogenannte historische Jesus und der geschichtliche biblische Christus*, 1892 — at a time when it cost something to say so — he

---

4. Albert Schweitzer, *The Quest of the Historical Jesus*, trans. W. Montgomery (London: Adam & Charles Black, 1910).

5. Henry Cadbury, *The Peril of Modernizing Jesus* (London: Macmillan, 1937).

6. Rudolf Bultmann, *Jesus and the Word*, trans. L. P. Smith and E. H. Lantero (New York: Scribner's, 1934) 8.

7. See Emil Brunner, *The Mediator: A Study of the Central Doctrine of the Christian Faith*, trans. Olive Wyon (Philadelphia: Westminster, 1947).

called the whole 'Life of Jesus movement' in plain language a 'wrong way.'"[8] Barth approved of Kähler's key idea "that the real historical Christ is no one other than the biblical Christ attested by the New Testament passages, i.e., the incarnate Word, the risen and exalted One.... There is no reason why historico-critical Bible research should not contribute to the investigation and exposition of this historical Christ of the New Testament, instead of ... chasing the ghost of an historical Jesus in the vacuum behind the New Testament."[9]

Søren Kierkegaard also influenced the dialectical theologians. He advanced the idea that faith cannot be dependent on the always fluctuating results of historical research. He asked, how can the probability knowledge of historical science provide the foundation of hope for eternal life? The dialectical theologians frequently quoted 2 Corinthians 5:16: "Even though we have known Christ after the flesh, yet now we know him so no more." The *Christus kata sarka* is the so-called historical Jesus of the historiographers, who profess to bracket out faith from their scholarly investigations. True, they bracket out biblical Christian faith. In its place they substitute their own rationalistic presuppositions or some other ideological commitments. The end product is a hypothetical Jesus, depicted as a mere man, and thus not the real Jesus, the historic, biblical Christ.

II. The Historical Jesus of the New Quest

The combined influence of the dialectical theologians, especially Barth and Bultmann, ensured that the quest of the historical Jesus would be placed on a back burner. The great systems of constructive theology for most of the twentieth century showed little interest in the Jesus research of technical scholarship. That was true not only of dialectical theology, but also of other types of theology: secularization theology, language analysis theology, process theology, as well as the confessional theologies of the various Christian traditions. Students parsed every neologism of the reigning philosophical thinkers—Heidegger, Sartre, Jaspers, Whitehead, and Wittgenstein—all of whom exercised enormous influence on various schools of theology.

Then something happened. The Bultmann school developed a heart murmur. Some of his former students feared that the patient was about

---

8. Karl Barth, *Church Dogmatics* I/2, trans. G. T. Thomson and Harold Knight (New York: Scribner's, 1956) 64.

9. Ibid., 64 and 65.

to die. Dr. Käsemann volunteered to perform the operation. In a famous article, "The Problem of the Historical Jesus,"[10] Käsemann reopened the quest of the historical Jesus. His goal was more modest than that of the biographical and psychological inquiries of the old quest. Käsemann feared that Bultmann's indifference to the historical Jesus would lead to docetism. Docetism was an ancient heresy that denied that Jesus was really a full-fledged human being. For Bultmann the historical Jesus possessed no constitutive significance for Christian faith in the exalted Lord, the kerygmatic Christ. For Käsemann it became a question of inescapable theological necessity to penetrate behind the kerygmatic Christ of apostolic preaching to establish continuity with the historical Jesus. He gave back to the historical critics the task of providing assurance based on credible evidence that the crucified and risen Lord—the very heart of the gospel—is identical with the earthly Jesus of Galilee. Otherwise, the ghost of docetism, Käsemann feared, would continue to haunt theology. The Easter faith would evaporate into the mythical Christ à la David Friedrich Strauss.

Käsemann's concern is theologically legitimate. We believe in one Lord Jesus Christ; the Jesus of Galilee is the risen Christ, the Lord of the Church. For Käsemann, the decisive question for faith is whether Jesus was the One whom the kerygma declared him to be. However, for Kähler, Barth, and Tillich, this is not a question that can be answered by historical research. Käsemann is asking the historian to do something that is theologically necessary, but way beyond his paygrade. Käsemann and his fellow new questers—Günther Bornkamm, Hans Conzelmann, Ernst Fuchs, Gerhard Ebeling, and others—managed to produce only new versions of a "so-called historical Jesus." Soon they were bypassed by the majority of New Testament theologians, and their influence on systematic theologians was negligible.

As for the charge of docetism, the very idea that modern historical criticism is needed to guarantee the true humanity of Jesus is absurd. The ancient church fathers defeated the heresy of docetism without any assistance from modern critical Jesus research. They constructed their arguments from the Scriptures as they are written, and not by going behind them to discover a purely human Jesus untouched by the titles of faith bestowed on him after Easter. Kähler's judgment is appropriate *vis-à-vis* the

---

10. Ernst Käsemann, "The Problem of the Historical Jesus," in *Essays on New Testament Themes* (London: SCM, 1964) 15–47.

Jesus of the new quest. It produces another version of the so-called historical Jesus, irrelevant to Christian faith and theology.

III. The Historical Jesus and the Real Jesus

Years flew by and I more or less forgot about Kähler and the quest of the historical Jesus, both the old quest and the new quest. I assumed that it had proved to be a dead end, and no serious scholar would venture down that path again. I was engaged in writing dogmatics, and although Christology was at the heart of it, the historical Jesus of the questers—whether old or new, positive or negative—was not. Then the floodgates opened and one scholar after another published a book on the historical Jesus. The quest was once again becoming big business. I started reading these books—dozens of them.

N. T. Wright coined the phrase the "third quest." Some of the Jesus books are written to prove that Christianity is false; others are written to prove that Christianity is true. What Yogi Berra said applies: "It's *déjà vu* all over again." History is repeating itself. I went to my library and dusted off all my old Kähler stuff, thesis and all. Just as I was asking, "Where is Kähler now that we need him?" I was pleased to discover that some of the leaders of the current quest readily concede Kähler's key observation: the reconstructed Jesus of modern historical scholarship is not the real Jesus. I refer to three scholars in particular: Luke Timothy Johnson, James D. G. Dunn, and John P. Meier. There are others, but I will cite these three historians in support of Kähler's thesis: the historical Jesus—the Jesus of modern historical scholarship—is not the real Jesus. The real Jesus is the living Christ of apostolic preaching, the risen Lord according to the testimonies[11] of the first Christians, who is still present as the world's Savior in the ongoing

---

11. Richard Bauckham, *Jesus and the Eyewitnesses: The Gospels as Eyewitness Testimony* (Grand Rapids: Eerdmans, 2006). What Bauckham says about the category of testimony resonates with Kähler's judgment. Bauckham writes, "Testimony, we will argue, is both the historically appropriate category for understanding what kind of history the Gospels are and the theologically appropriate category for understanding what kind of access Christian readers of the Gospels thereby have to Jesus and his history. It is the category that enables us to surmount the dichotomy between the so-called historical Jesus and the so-called Christ of faith. It enables us to see that the Gospels are not some kind of obstacle to knowledge of the real Jesus and his history but precisely the kind of means of access to the real Jesus and his history that, as historians and as believers, we need" (473).

experience of the church. The Gospels tell the story of the incarnate life of this risen, living Lord.

Here is a sample of what these scholars are saying.

Luke Timothy Johnson, a New Testament scholar at Emory University, writes, "Even the best historical reconstruction cannot supply the 'real Jesus'.... The 'real Jesus' for Christian faith is the resurrected Jesus.... The real Jesus is not simply a figure of the past but very much and above all a figure of the present."[12] Johnson continues:

> The premise of the last search as for the first is: the only way to find the "real Jesus" is to bypass the Jesus found in the canonical Gospels.... The Historical Jesus researchers insist that the "real Jesus" must be found in the facts of his life before his death.... Their operative premise is that there is no "real Jesus" after his death.... Christians, when they are consistent with their own classical tradition, take the exact opposite position: the "real Jesus" is the one who is now alive, and powerfully present, through the Holy Spirit, in the world and in the lives of human beings.... From the perspective of Christian faith in the resurrected Lord, any claim to capture the "real Jesus" that stops short of his resurrection is wildly wrongheaded.[13]

Otherwise put, "Corresponding to the Christian claim, there is a 'real Jesus' in the texts of the New Testament as they have been transmitted to this generation."[14]

James D. G. Dunn, a prolific Jesus researcher at the University of Durham, England, agrees with Johnson. He writes, "We must recognize the fallacy of thinking that the real Jesus must be a nonfaith Jesus, different from the Jesus of the Gospels."[15] "There is no credible 'historical Jesus' behind the Gospel portrayal different from the characteristic Jesus of the Synoptic tradition. But this assuredly is the historical Jesus that the Christian wants to encounter. And should the scholar and historian be content with anything less?"[16] Dunn goes on: "It is here that Kähler's key observation needs to

---

12. Luke Timothy Johnson, *The Real Jesus: The Misguided Quest for the Historical Jesus and the Truth of the Traditional Gospels* (HarperCollins: HarperSanFrancisco, 1996) 141, 142.

13. Ibid., 144.

14. Ibid., 167.

15. *A New Perspective on Jesus: What the Quest for the Historical Jesus Missed* (Grand Rapids: Baker Academic) 22.

16. Ibid., 78.

be reasserted. The idea that a Jesus reconstructed from the Gospel traditions . . . is the same Jesus who taught in Galilee . . . is an illusion. The idea that we can see through the faith perspective of the New Testament writings to a Jesus who did not inspire faith or who inspired faith in a different way is an illusion. There is no such Jesus. That there was a Jesus who did inspire faith which in due course found expression in the Gospels is not in question. But that we can somehow hope to strip out the theological impact which he actually made on his disciples, to uncover a different Jesus (the real Jesus!), is at best fanciful."[17]

John P. Meier, professor of New Testament at the University of Notre Dame, has written more on the historical Jesus than any scholar since the Enlightenment. Yet he concedes that despite all his labor, using the strictest canons of historical critical research, he has not reached the real Jesus. He writes, "The historical Jesus is not the real Jesus. The real Jesus is not the historical Jesus."[18]

Meier continues: "Having abandoned the naive hope of knowing the 'real' Jesus by means of historical criticism, what do we mean when we say that we are pursuing the 'historical Jesus' or the 'Jesus of history'? . . . By the Jesus of history I mean the Jesus whom we can 'recover' and examine by using the scientific tools of modern historical research."[19] If the guild of biblical scholars who use the historical-critical method cannot deliver the goods on the real Jesus, then how do we gain access to him? Meier believes that the task of theology is to reflect on the knowledge of faith. The historical critic does not work from a faith perspective. The theologian starts from the standpoint of the believer. His or her reflections will occur within a conceptual framework shaped by belief in the triune God and the risen Jesus.[20] Thus Meier concludes, stating his agreement with Kähler, "the Jesus of history is not and cannot be the object of Christian faith."[21] The reasons for this are as obvious to Meier as they were to Kähler, Barth, and Tillich. For eighteen hundred years Christians believed in the person of Jesus Christ without depending on the results of modern critical historical research. Moreover, there is no consensus among modern historians as

17. James D. G. Dunn, *Jesus Remembered* (Grand Rapids: Eerdmans, 2003) 126.
18. John P. Meier, *A Marginal Jew: Rethinking the Historical Jesus*, vol. 1, *The Roots of the Problem and the Person* (New York: Doubleday, 1991) 21.
19. Ibid., 25.
20. Ibid., 197.
21. Ibid.

to who Jesus was. Meier asks, "*Whose* historical Jesus would be the object of faith? Albert Schweitzer's or Eduard Schweitzer's? Herbert Braun's or Joachim Jeremias's? Günther Bornkamm's or E. P. Sanders'? Jesus the violent revolutionary or Jesus the gay magician? Jesus the apocalyptic seer or Jesus the wisdom teacher unconcerned with eschatology? The constantly changing, often contradictory portraits of the historical Jesus served up by scholars, however useful in academia, cannot be the object of Christian faith for the universal Church."[22]

Putting on the hat of a theologian, Meier states, "For the believer, the object of Christian faith is a living person, Jesus Christ, who fully entered into a true human existence on earth in the first century A.D., but who now lives, risen and glorified, forever in the Father's presence.... In the realm of faith and theology, the 'real Jesus,' the only Jesus existing and living now, is the risen Jesus, to whom access is given only through faith."[23]

These three big guns of New Testament scholarship—Johnson, Dunn, and Meier (sounds like a law firm)—agree that the historical-critical method does not result in gaining access to the real Jesus. However, for them that need not put an end to historical Jesus research. They engage in it full time. They believe that theologians are wise to keep themselves informed about what scholars are saying about the historical Jesus, although what they will learn for certain is anything but certain.

We already know from a plain-sense reading of the Gospels what the majority of scholars can agree on. E. P. Sanders draws up a list of about twelve things: 1) Jesus was born around 4 BCE; 2) he grew up in Nazareth, a village in Galilee; 3) he was baptized by John the Baptist; 4) he called disciples; 5) he taught in towns and villages in Galilee; 6) he preached the kingdom of God; 7) he went to Jerusalem for Passover around 30 CE; 8) he created a disturbance in the Temple area; 9) he had a final meal with the disciples; 10) he was arrested and interrogated by Jewish authorities; 11) he was crucified on the orders of Pontius Pilate; and 12) his disciples fled, and some claimed to have seen him a short time later.[24] That is a list on which scholars can agree. And it's exactly what most of us learned in Sunday school. Beyond that they do not agree on much. They do not come close to agreeing on who Jesus thought he was, nor on what he meant by the kingdom of God. This lack of agreement may underscore that when

22. Ibid., 198.
23. Ibid.
24. E. P. Sanders, *The Historical Figure of Jesus* (London: Penguin, 1993) 10–11.

it comes to the figure of Jesus, the principle of analogy breaks down. If Jesus is really the one whom the apostles and evangelists proclaimed him to be, using as they did a plethora of high christological titles, then he was truly unique. It is not surprising that someone who is both God and man eludes all our usual categories to portray the lives and thoughts of the great personages of history.

IV. Christian Faith and the Historical Method

We have barely touched the surface of the hermeneutical problem of how to relate the historical and theological disciplines. John Meier's approach tends to keep historical reason and Christian faith completely separate. He asks his Catholic readers not to get upset with him for "holding to a strict distinction between what I know about Jesus by research and reason and what I hold by faith."[25] The Germans have a word for that: *zweigleisigkeit*—two tracks, two parallel rails running side by side that never meet.

Another approach is to insist on pursuing one track, riding a monorail. That is the approach of the "Jesus Seminar," judging by the writings of its leaders, Robert W. Funk and John Dominic Crossan. For both of them the only real Jesus is the reconstructed Jesus of contemporary scholarship. John Dominic Crossan concludes his tome on the historical Jesus with these words: "One cannot dismiss . . . the search for the historical Jesus as mere reconstruction, as if reconstruction invalidated somehow the entire project. Because there is only reconstruction. . . . If you cannot believe in something produced by reconstruction, you may have nothing left to believe in."[26] For Crossan, the real Jesus is *his* reconstructed Jesus, and our only means of access to such a Jesus is by historical-critical research.

Robert W. Funk, the founder of the "Jesus Seminar" in 1985, set out in search of the real Jesus with the stated purpose of overthrowing the Christology of traditional Christianity. He wrote, "It is a good thing that the true historical Jesus should overthrow the Christ of Christian orthodoxy, the Christ of the creeds. . . . The aim of the quest of the historical Jesus is to set Jesus free, to liberate him from the prevailing captivities."[27] The captivity he

---

25. Ibid., 6.

26. John Dominic Crossan, *The Historical Jesus: The Life of a Mediterranean Jewish Peasant* (Harper Collins: HarperSanFrancisco, 1992) 426.

27. Robert W. Funk, *Honest to Jesus: Jesus for a New Millennium* (HarperCollins: HarperSanFrancisco, 1996) 20, 21.

identifies is not merely the creeds of Nicaea and Chalcedon, but also the Gospels. Funk writes, "Even the Christ of the Gospels is an impediment to any serious effort to rediscover Jesus of Nazareth."[28] The whole New Testament is not to be trusted, because it was written by people who believed in Jesus. Funk writes, "We can no longer rest our faith on the faith of Peter or the faith of Paul. I do not want my faith to be a secondhand faith. . . . Jesus himself is not the proper object of faith. . . . I do not want to be misled by what his [Jesus'] followers did; instead of looking to see what he saw, his devoted disciples tended to stare at the pointing finger. Jesus himself should not be, must not be, the object of faith. That would be to repeat the idolatry of the first believers."[29] The leaders of the "Jesus Seminar" make no bones about it. The aim of their Jesus research is to replace Christianity with a new religion. In this respect they revive the hostility of the eighteenth-century rationalistic critics toward the Christology of classical Christianity.

However, it is not only the neoliberal questers of the "Jesus Seminar" who believe that they can discover the real Jesus by the historical-critical method. Some conservatives also seem to believe the same thing. Tom Wright[30] leads the group, but others can be mentioned, such as Ben Witherington III,[31] Craig L. Blomberg,[32] and Craig A. Evans.[33] I call them conservatives because their use of the historical method aims to discover a Jesus more compatible with the New Testament picture of Christ as a whole, as well as with the Christ of traditional Christian worship. These and many others whom I have not cited widen the field strewn with the debris of theses and countertheses, arguments and counterarguments, and even name-calling. Funk calls Meier a "blockhead."[34] Craig dismisses the scholarship of current Jesus researchers as "hokum history" and "bogus research."[35] Unflattering comments are hurled back and forth with emotional intensity.

28. Ibid., 20.

29. Ibid., 304, 305.

30. N. T. Wright, *Christian Origins and the Question of God*, vol. 2, *Jesus and the Victory of God* (Minneapolis: Fortress, 1996).

31. Ben Witherington III, *The Jesus Quest: The Third Search for the Jew of Nazareth* (Downers Grove, IL: InterVarsity, 1995).

32. Craig L. Blomberg, *The Historical Reliability of the Gospels* (Downers Grove, IL: InterVarsity, 1987).

33. Craig A. Evans, *Fabricating Jesus: How Modern Scholars Distort the Gospels* (Downers Grove, IL: InterVarsity, 2006).

34. Mark Allan Powell, *Jesus as a Figure of History: How Modern Historians View the Man from Galilee* (Louisville: Westminster John Knox, 1998) 76.

35. Evans, *Fabricating Jesus*, 222.

Who Do You Say That I Am?

Negative critics reject, and positive critics defend, traditional Christian faith. If you have read only a fraction of the Jesus books, you may have felt like Mary Magdalene outside the tomb on Easter morning. She said to the risen Jesus, "They have taken away my Lord, and I do not know where they have laid him" (John 20:13).

V. The Theologian's Quandary

We are fortunate to have one of the front-ranking Jesus scholars on our CCET program this year, Dale Allison. He has written extensively on New Testament themes, even several books on the historical Jesus. Since he speaks tomorrow, he is in the position to correct what I have to say. So far I have taken the position, supported by some theologians and historians, that the historical-critical method is incapable of providing access to the real Jesus. I believe Dale Allison's book *The Historical Christ and the Theological Jesus* says a number of things that comport with such a perspective. He observes that scholars do not agree "regarding most of the truly interesting and theologically charged questions."[36] In particular, there is no agreement in answer to the question, who was Jesus? Allison writes:

> More than one historical Jesus resides between today's book covers. We indeed have a plethora of them. There is the Jesus of Tom Wright, a Jewish prophet and almost, it seems, orthodox Christian. There is the Jesus of Marcus Borg, a religious mystic who dispensed perennial wisdom. There is the Jesus of E. P. Sanders, a Jewish eschatological prophet à la Albert Schweitzer. There is the Jesus of John Dominic Crossan, a Galilean but Cynic-like peasant whose vision of an egalitarian kingdom and non-violent God stood in stark contrast to the power politics of Roman domination. One could go on. To the outsider, theories about Jesus must seem to crisscross each other to create a maze of contradictions.[37]

The result is that "the Jesus of one book often does not look much like the Jesus of another book, even when those books employ more or less the same method."[38]

---

36. Dale C. Allison, Jr., *The Historical Christ and the Theological Jesus* (Grand Rapids: Eerdmans, 2009) 9.

37. Ibid., 8.

38. Ibid., 57.

Allison rightly asserts that "any contemporary theology that takes its bearing from contemporary reconstructions of the historical Jesus will be defunct as soon as those reconstructions become defunct, which will not be very long."[39] That puts theologians in a sort of a quandary, Allison says:

> They can do one of three things. First, they can rely on their dated knowledge, gleaned during their school days, of what New Testament scholars have written about Jesus. This will guarantee that on some important matters they will be holding judgments that have since been revised or abandoned. Second, they can attempt to acquaint themselves with contemporary work. In this case, they will manage to sample only some of what is out there, and they will be faced, as just observed, with the arduous task of deciding, as amateurs, which purported authorities are right and which are wrong. Third, they can simply go on their own way and ignore the quest as a matter of indifference, remaining undisturbed in their theological convictions, hoping or believing that nothing much important has been or is going on, or at least nothing much religiously important.[40]

Is the theologian really stuck in such a quandary with no way out? Might it be that those are not the only three options? A fourth option would start with Kähler's premise that the quest of the historical Jesus is on the wrong track, that it does not deliver the real Jesus. Therefore, the theologian does not need to join the hunt for the historical Jesus behind the canonical Gospels. I believe this was the path taken by theologians such as Martin Kähler, Karl Barth, and Wolfhart Pannenberg. This approach is now endorsed, as we have shown, by such New Testament scholars as John Meier, James Dunn, and Luke Timothy Johnson. I think I am correct in observing that this approach is more or less represented by the study group sponsored by the Center of Theological Inquiry that resulted in a publication titled *Seeking the Identity of Jesus*, edited by Beverly R. Gaventa and Richard B. Hays.[41] These scholars acknowledge that the real identity of Jesus is bound up with his reception as the Christ, with the impact he made on those who remembered him. It is impossible to know who Jesus really is apart from participating in the life of the church, the body of which he is the head.

So what is the theological significance of a reconstructed Jesus, the hypothetical Jesus of historical criticism? I can't think of any, except that it

---

39. Ibid., 10.
40. Ibid., 14.
41. *Seeking the Identity of Jesus: A Pilgrimage* (Grand Rapids: Eerdmans, 2008).

shows that the majority of scholars assume that whoever Jesus really was, he really did exist in time and space and is therefore in principle subject to historical investigation as much as other figures of ancient history. So I am asking, have we gotten ourselves out of the quandary?

VI. The Means of Access to the Real Jesus

The quest of the historical Jesus was a project of the Enlightenment. Hermann Samuel Reimarus, a professor of Oriental languages in Germany, is usually credited with having initiated the historical investigation into the life of Jesus around the middle of the eighteenth century. Much like Robert Funk of the "Jesus Seminar," his aim was to drive a wedge between Jesus and Christianity. He was much in favor of the moral teachings of Jesus that passed the test of enlightened reason, but opposed to the christological dogmas of the ancient church. Immanuel Kant gave further impetus to this view of Jesus as a moral example for everyone to follow. Miracles and mystery are ruled out of Kant's "religion within the limits of reason alone."[42] The nineteenth-century quest of the historical Jesus was carried out in accordance with the principles of a natural religion of reason. From this point of departure there is no way to move from the historical Jesus so constructed to the Christology of the church and the doctrine of the triune God.

Kant's influence led to a deistic concept of God and an ebionitic image of Jesus. However, there was another line of thinking coming out of the Enlightenment that offered greater promise to church theologians who wished to retain continuity with the christological and Trinitarian dogmas of classical Christianity. Both F. W. J. Schelling and G. W. F. Hegel inspired new initiatives in rethinking Christology and the doctrine of the Trinity. Such rethinking did not depend on the "back to Jesus" research, nor did it call for outright rejection of the classical dogmas.[43] Some theologians agreed with this approach, such as Philipp K. Marheineke, Alois Emanuel Biedermann, Gottfried Thomasius, and Isaak August Dorner. For them what is important about Jesus was not his role as a teacher of morality but the presence of

---

42. This is the title of Kant's most influential book on religion, written after his major philosophical critiques.

43. For a lengthy treatise on Hegel's contribution to Protestant theology in the nineteenth century, see Hans Küng, *The Incarnation of God: An Introduction to Hegel's Thought as Prolegomena to a Future Christology*, trans. J. R. Stephenson (London: T. & T. Clark, 1987).

God in him. For Kant, God and man are separate. The finite is not capable of the infinite. For Hegel, God and man are united in the person of Jesus. The infinite is capable of the finite. For the Kantian side of Enlightenment religion, there can be no real incarnation of God. For the theologians who took their cue from Schelling or Hegel, the incarnation of God in Jesus is what Christianity is all about. And that is the essence of classical Christology, whatever other details needed to be worked out. The line of thought following Reimarus and Kant produced images of Jesus incompatible with a real incarnation, which in fact was their intention.

The question, "Who is the real Jesus?" will be answered quite differently depending on whether one believes that Jesus was a godlike man or rather the very being of God appearing in history as a man. In the former case Jesus is a good man on the same level as Socrates; in the latter case Jesus is the God-man, the incarnate Son of God, and therefore without equal.

Where does one get the idea that Jesus was a mere man? Not from the Gospels as we have them, but rather by subtracting from the Gospels everything that testifies to his uniqueness. The "Jesus Seminar" calculates that after such a process of subtraction, only about 18 percent of the Synoptic Gospels can be regarded as authentic—that is, they accurately report the very words and deeds of Jesus. Virtually nothing in the Gospel of John meets the test. The percentage varies from quester to quester, but the result in the end is the same. Jesus is pictured one way or another as a godlike man rather than as the incarnation of God. So we can put the shoe on the other foot and ask, Where does one get the idea that Jesus is more than a man, that he is really God, that the life of the human historical Jesus is the history of God himself?

Such a belief is based on the Gospels and the New Testament as a whole, indeed, the whole of Scripture. The real Jesus is portrayed as the risen Christ, alive and present where his body is, namely, where his people are, the community of believers, the church. For the mainstream of the Christian tradition the only way to meet the real Jesus is through the preaching of the Word of God, mediated by the sacred Scriptures, within the community of believers, and empowered by the Holy Spirit. This sounds like Sunday school stuff—the sort of stuff with which Christian theologians in fact do work. I do not know any dogmatic theologians who base their thinking about Christ on the historical Jesus as reconstructed by scholars who peel away the layers of written and oral traditions that presumably lie behind the Gospels. The real Jesus who is God for us remains hidden to all who do not come to him with a living personal faith. The knowledge of faith born of the Spirit is accessible to ordinary laypersons. It is not a work of the intellect that only skilled practitioners of historical research can perform.

This is the hermeneutical significance of the doctrine of justification by faith, the hallmark of a theology of salvation that both Protestants and Catholics confess they share in common.[44] Genuine Christian knowledge of God presupposes a living faith in Jesus as the risen Christ. This is a knowledge unmediated by the results of the modern search for the historical Jesus. A reconstructed image of the historical Jesus separated from his picture as the Christ of God in the Gospels is not only a dubious historico-scientific enterprise, it is also of no apologetic value or theological significance. None of the three quests of the historical Jesus provides faith the means of access to the revelation of God incarnate in the person of Jesus Christ.

This negative verdict does not mean that the modern historical-critical method is of no value to Christian theology. The modern methods of historical criticism used in the study of the Bible are here to stay. We could not turn back the clock to a precritical period of biblical theology if we tried. One of the best things written on this topic that I know of is the 1993 statement produced by the Pontifical Biblical Commission titled *The Interpretation of the Bible in the Church*. It fully endorses the historical-critical method, but not its use in quest of a Jesus excavated from somewhere behind the texts of the canonical Gospels. That is a project of the unenlightened side of the Enlightenment that began with Herman Samuel Reimarus and continues apace, with the same skeptical spirit, in the "Jesus Seminar." It never gets beyond seeing Jesus as a mere man; its Christology is ebionitic. In fact, *Christology* is not the right term, because its Jesus is radically non-Messianic. Many of the questers—certainly not all—use their image of Jesus to settle a score with the institutional church and its dogmatic teachings about Christ. This is most conspicuously the case with Marcus Borg's writings on Jesus.[45] In his book *Meeting Jesus Again for the First Time*, Borg

---

44. On October 31, 1999, Catholics and Lutherans signed the Joint Declaration on the Doctrine of Justification, thus burying the hatchet on their chief point of difference since the sixteenth century.

45. Marcus J. Borg, *Jesus, A New Vision: Spirit, Culture, and the Life of Discipleship* (San Francisco: Harper & Row, 1987); Borg, *Meeting Jesus Again for the First Time: The Historical Jesus and the Heart of Contemporary Faith* (HarperCollins: HarperSanFrancisco, 1994). John Dominic Crossan's image of Jesus is also slanted to attack the magisterial teachings and structures of the Roman Catholic Church with which he disagrees as a former priest. See his *Jesus: A Revolutionary Biography* (HarperCollins: HarperSanFrancisco, 1994).

tells about how, growing up in a Lutheran church in North Dakota, he was taught to believe that Jesus was God, the Savior of the world. Now, having advanced to what he calls "a mature faith," he realizes that the historical figure of Jesus was very different from the way the Gospels and Christian tradition speak of him.[46]

This is my view: the means of access to the real Jesus can be fully expounded only on the basis of propositions borrowed from Christian dogmatics. Every scholar approaches ancient texts with a set of presuppositions, although some scholars pretend they have none. The following are mine.

1. Apart from faith there can be no knowledge of God's self-revelation in the person of Jesus as the Christ. A faith perspective is fully compatible with a robust use of reason in historical inquiry. Reason needs faith as the power of its vision. Apart from faith reason is blind, and apart from reason faith is empty, to paraphrase Kant's famous formula. What reason sees is made possible by faith.

2. Faith is made possible by the witness of the Holy Spirit, a gift of God alone. Faith's acceptance of the biblical portrayal of the identity and meaning of Jesus Christ is brought about by the inspiration of the Holy Spirit.

3. The Holy Spirit of God the Father and the Lord Jesus Christ works through the means of grace, through the audible words of preaching and the visible words of the sacraments. The risen Jesus becomes real in the experience of faith by means of the living voice of the gospel through the power of the Holy Spirit.

4. The preaching of Jesus Christ that awakens faith is performed by the church and its ministries, and none other. Outside the church there is no gospel of salvation that draws its spiritual power from the crucified and resurrected Jesus. The church is God's chosen instrument and sacrament, communicating what his Holy Spirit is doing in the world.

These factors of faith—Scripture, Spirit, and church—are links in a hermeneutical chain that connects the living, risen Jesus to the witnessing and worshipping community of Christ today.

---

46. Borg, *Meeting Jesus Again for the First Time*, 10, 15, 37, 136.

VII. The Historicity of God Incarnate

The modern historical research into the life of Jesus has produced many Jesuses, yielding no consensus on which to construct a Christology. Nevertheless, the persistent study of the sources to discover what really happened in history has had a positive effect not only on the way theologians stress the historicity of Jesus but also on the way they think of God. As we have said, a core confession of Christian faith is that Jesus of Nazareth is the incarnation of God. The struggles of the ancient church on the way to Nicaea and Chalcedon brooked no abbreviation of the true humanity and true divinity of the person of Jesus Christ. The confession of John that "the Word became flesh" (John 1:14) and of Paul that "God was in Christ" (2 Cor 5:19) embedded God in the history and destiny of a human being. Contemporary systematic theologians speak of God in radically human terms, using language like the "humanity of God" or the "historicity of God." They are freeing the confession of Jesus as "true God and true man" from its association with the Greek metaphysical idea of an immutable, impassible, and immortal God. Starting with the historicity of Jesus, the logic of the incarnation leads to the concept of the historicity of God. Put it this way: it just doesn't work to incarnate a Greek or Gnostic deity in a Jewish Jesus.[47] If we take seriously the historicity of God's self-investment in Jesus, we will abandon some assumptions about God that are more at home in Athens than in Jerusalem. In Greek metaphysics and Hellenistic religion the eternal God had of necessity to be essentially immortal, impassible, and immutable. In other words, God could not die, God could not suffer, God could not change. But change, suffering, and death are the common lot of every human being, including Jesus. If we take seriously the Gospel narrative that Jesus is God in the flesh, then He did enter into the changing conditions of human existence, He did know what it means to suffer, and He did experience the reality of death. The idea of an absolutely immutable, impassible, and immortal God may fit the metaphysics of pagan antiquity and New Age mysticism, but it does not cohere with the living God of the Old and New Testaments.[48]

---

47. See the important article by Wolfhart Pannenberg, "The Appropriation of the Philosophical Concept of God as a Dogmatic Problem of Early Christian Theology," in *Basic Questions in Theology*, vol. 2, trans. George H. Kehm (Philadelphia: Fortress, 1971) 119–83.

48. To plumb the depths of this theological shift to a historicist understanding of the incarnation of God in the person of Jesus Christ, one must read the books of Karl Barth,

Conclusion

The critics of the position that I am defending will be legion, some historians and some theologians. They will likely charge that this position does not take history seriously, that it is a flight into docetism, that it seeks to make faith invulnerable to the assured results of historical science. They will likely say—reaching for a clinching theological argument—that since Christians believe that God revealed himself in the life and teachings of a particular human being, they must be committed to the quest of the historical Jesus.

Our counterargument is that the problem with the quest is not only its christological deficit, but also its failure to take history seriously. After all, what is history? A historical event is not reducible to a bare-naked fact—a kind of Kantian "*ding an sich*"—minus its influence, its perceived meaning. The real Jesus of history is not a Jesus minus his effect on the disciples before his resurrection and on the apostles and evangelists after Easter. Hans-Georg Gadamer's concept of *Wirkungsgeschichte*[49] (effective history) offers a useful background theory to describe the full meaning of a historical event. The real Jesus is not merely Jesus stripped of his identity as the Christ. His Christ-ness is part of who he really is, and to know this to be true involves a confession of faith simply unavailable to historical criticism. His true identity in history is bound up with those who believed in him, who confessed him as their Lord and Savior, and who remembered him in ways completely different from other contemporaries. The Four Gospels present such a picture of Jesus as the Christ of God, and we have no need to look for another by deconstructing the Gospels.

N. T. Wright is one who takes objection to our thesis that the real Jesus is not the reconstructed Jesus of the questers. He writes, "The way to find the real Jesus is, as it were, by a pincer movement: forwards from the picture of first-century Judaism; backwards from the Gospels."[50] He agrees with his fellow questers that it is necessary to go behind the Gospels to find the real Jesus. He writes, "I totally agree with the proposals of the sceptical 'questers,' from Reimarus right down to A. N. Wilson. It is not only possible, but actually highly likely, that the church has distorted the

---

Eberhard Jüngel, Wolfhart Pannenberg, Jürgen Moltmann, Hans Urs von Balthasar, Walter Kasper, and Robert W. Jenson.

49. Hans-Georg Gadamer, *Truth and Method*, trans. J. Weinsheimer and D. G. Marshall (New York: Crossroad, 1989).

50. N. T. Wright, *Who Was Jesus?* (Grand Rapids: Eerdmans, 1992) 95.

real Jesus, and needs to repent of this and rediscover who its Lord actually is."[51] He says, "They [the questers] address the right issue, namely, who Jesus really was—as opposed to who the church has imagined him to be."[52] Wright's problem with all the other questers whom he criticizes is not their goal to find the real Jesus of history, but that "they fail to reach anything like the right answer."[53] He says, "They have offered us a Jesus of their own imagination."[54] We are left to believe that only Wright gets it right.

I have shared my conviction that today we are in a situation like unto the one in which Martin Kähler found himself. Surveying the history of the quest, he reached a conclusion that Schweitzer could not: "The historical Jesus of the modern authors conceals from us the living Christ. . . . I regard the entire Life-of-Jesus movement as a blind alley. . . . The risen Lord is not the historical Jesus behind the Gospels, but the Christ of the apostolic preaching, of the whole New Testament."[55] Schweitzer believed that the history of the quest was a failure; he thought he could set it straight. Wright believes that Schweitzer's picture of the apocalyptic Jesus was wrong, and so is every other scholarly picture of the historical Jesus, until the big breakthrough, the rescue operation of Wright's "third quest." This approach also fails to provide adequate access to the real historic, biblical Christ, the whole Christ of the whole Bible, on which the classical Christology of the church is founded.[56]

---

51. Ibid., 18.

52. Ibid., viii.

53. Ibid.

54. Ibid., 18.

55. Kähler, *The So-Called Historical Jesus and the Historic, Biblical Christ*, 43, 46, 65.

56. In his book *Simply Christian: Why Christianity Makes Sense* (HarperCollins: HarperSanFrancisco, 2006), N. T. Wright writes as an apologetic theologian, explaining the essence of Christianity. It reminds one of C. S. Lewis' *Mere Christianity*, but N. T. Wright is no C. S. Lewis. His doctrine of the Trinity and his Christology seem to me to be pusillanimous approximations of the robust doxological affirmations of Nicaea and Chalcedon.

2

Jesus and the Historians

Dale C. Allison, Jr.

I REMEMBER THE DAY, or rather the evening, when I set out on the quest for the historical Jesus. I was seventeen years old and sitting, with half a dozen teenagers, in the small library of a Methodist church. We were studying the Bible. When our work was done, my eyes wandered around the shelves. They happened to fall upon a worn hardback, an old copy of Albert Schweitzer's *The Quest of the Historical Jesus*.[1]

I had first heard of Schweitzer while sitting in another church, almost a decade earlier. Schweitzer had just died—it was 1965—and a nice old lady, a Baptist Sunday school teacher, oblivious of his heretical theology, was holding him up to us little ones as a moral exemplar, praising his work as a medical missionary in Africa. So when, years later, I saw his name on a book spine, I knew enough to realize that Schweitzer was supposed to be a great man. I picked up his *Quest*, and I read it.

Schweitzer introduced me to a spellbinding albeit often confusing world, one I have lived in ever since. He documented, in entertaining fashion, and often with flowery prose, the efforts of scholars, mostly German, to ascertain how much history is in the canonical gospels, and how that history should be interpreted. I was, for reasons I do not fully understand, hypnotized, and it was not long before I was searching for more of the same

---

1. Albert Schweitzer, *The Quest of the Historical Jesus: A Critical Study of Its Progress from Reimarus to Wrede*, 2nd Eng. ed. (London: A. & C. Black, 1931).

in the stacks of the local public library, and then later in the stacks of the local state university. I read everything I could find on the subject. It all seemed, back then, so important, so revelatory—in part, I suppose, because nobody had ever dropped a hint to me that such a critical endeavor existed. It was as though I had broken into the mysterious Vatican basement and discovered the unedifying secrets hidden from the masses. My parents, my Sunday school teachers, and my pastors had said nothing about this.

In any event, I soon became acquainted also with the many scholars who, after Schweitzer, shared his aspiration to unearth the historical, the supposedly real Jesus. Their books and articles enthralled me so much that I ended up in a PhD program in New Testament studies and eventually, for good or ill, wrote my own books on the subject, which presumably is why I am here today.

What exactly is this so-called quest that Schweitzer chronicled and that academics since his day have continued to take up? It marks a departure from traditional Christian discourse, which for the most part equated the gospels with history. The European deists, who rejected that equation, set things in motion. Their disbelief in miracles required new readings of the Bible. How do you explain narratives full of miracles when you are sure that miracles do not happen? This was, for instance, the chief issue for Hermann Samuel Reimarus, the eighteenth-century German pastor with whom Schweitzer began his retrospective. Reimarus decided that Jesus was not the miracle-working Son of God but a would-be Jewish messiah who expected to rule as a militant king in Jerusalem. When he failed, his duplicitous followers, disinclined to go back to common labor, invented his resurrection and continued in ministry.[2]

It is not my purpose today to review for you the story of the quest from Reimarus forward. For that, I can happily commend to you Schweitzer and, for more recent work, subsequent cartographers of the discipline.[3] It is also not my goal to offer an overview of most of the big questions, historical and theological, that have driven and accompanied the quest. I will not, for instance, ask what we should make of the miracles in the gospels, which for so many have become not evidence of Jesus' exalted status but reason to doubt the historicity of our sources. Nor shall I address the complex and

---

2. Hermann Samuel Reimarus, *Fragments*, ed. Charles H. Talbert (Philadelphia: Fortress, 1970).

3. Esp. useful is Walter P. Weaver, *The Historical Jesus in the Twentieth Century, 1900–1950* (Harrisburg, PA: Trinity, 1999).

mysterious character of the Gospel of John, which is so different in so many significant ways from the other canonical gospels. I will also abstain from asking how much attention theologians should pay to Schweitzer and his ilk, whose various and conflicting reconstructions of the historical Jesus come and go with such rapidity.

Although fascinating and important, these are not my issues today. I rather wish to offer four large generalizations about the quest. The first two generalizations have to do with what historians cannot do, even if they have vainly imagined otherwise. The third and fourth generalizations are about what historians can do—or rather what they have, in my judgment, already done.

So then to my first sweeping statement: all attempts to fashion a historical Jesus too different from the synoptic Jesus have hitherto failed, and all such future attempts will likewise fail. To clarify what I mean, let me introduce you to a prominent and influential historian of Jesus with whom I have substantial disagreements. The late Robert Funk, cofounder of the Jesus Seminar, argued at length that traditional Christology has no real basis in the pre-Easter Jesus. Jesus of Nazareth may have referred to himself as "the Son of Man," but the expression, Funk held, was just a common Aramaic idiom, more or less as a pronoun. So when Jesus spoke of himself as "the Son of Man," it had nothing to do with Daniel's vision of the last judgment, where one like a son of man comes on the clouds of heaven. Nor did Jesus think of himself as the Messiah in any sense. Nor as the Son of God in any unique sense. In fact, he did not see himself as playing any special role in divine or human history. In Funk's words, the real Jesus "had nothing to say about himself, other than that he had no permanent address, no bed to sleep in, no respect on his home turf."[4]

Such a conclusion is so provocative—and it is designed to be provocative—in large measure because the Jesus of the Gospels—not just of John but of the Synoptics, too—has a great deal to say about himself. He calls himself "Lord" and warns that not to do what he commands will bring personal destruction (Matt 7:21–27 = Luke 6:46–49). He declares that the fate of at least some individuals at the final assize will depend upon whether they have confessed him or denied him (Mark 8:38; Matt 10:32–33 = Luke 12:8–9). He interprets his success in casting out demons "by the finger of God" to mean that God's kingdom has arrived, thereby making himself

---

4. Robert W. Funk, *Honest to Jesus: Jesus for a New Millennium* (San Francisco: HarperSanFrancisco, 1996) 41.

out to be the chief means or manifestation of its arrival (Matt 12:28 = Luke 11:20). He says that no one knows the Father except the Son and those to whom the Son reveals him (Matt 11:27 = Luke 10:22). He prophesies that cities not welcoming him will suffer for it at the eschatological judgment (Matt 10:15; 11:21–24 = Luke 10:12–15). He reads from the beginning of Isaiah 61 and proclaims that its prophecies are fulfilled in his ministry (Luke 4:16–19). He teaches that people who "receive" the disciples really "receive" him, and adds that to "receive" him is to receive the one who sent him (Matt 10:40 = Luke 10:16). And he foretells that he will someday return and send angels to gather the elect from throughout the world (Mark 13:26–27; cf. 14:62; Matt 10:23). In short—and even if, as I have just done, one sets John aside—the literary Jesus not only says a lot about himself but owns quite an exalted self-conception. He is not just God's definitive prophetic envoy but the locus of the whole eschatological scenario, and above all the central figure of the last judgment.

Given the relevant materials, how does Funk come to his uncanonical conclusions? His method is pretty standard. It is one of subtraction and reconfiguration. He first goes through the tradition and, wielding widely used criteria, excises numerous items—in fact, most items—as later additions. He then interprets what remains in a way that often goes against the primary sources, giving us a Jesus who could never say much or indeed most of what he says in Matthew, Mark, Luke, and John.

What is wrong with this procedure? For one thing, it depends upon the reliability of the so-called criteria of authenticity. These are surgical instruments designed to help scholars remove the post-Easter addenda from the pre-Easter Jesus. Over the past fifty years, they have been the tools of choice for most academics questing for the Jesus of history. One understands why. Upon initial consideration, the criteria do not seem so bad. The criterion of dissimilarity reckons traditions to be authentic when they differ from characteristic emphases of early Judaism and early Christianity. Where is the logical flaw in that? The criterion of multiple attestation holds that the more sources in which an item appears, the greater the odds it is from Jesus. Is this not one of the fundamental principles of sound journalism? The criterion of embarrassment has it that a particular saying or event that early Christians found less than congenial likely goes back to Jesus. Who could find that objectionable? The criterion of coherence has it that we may reckon authentic items that cohere with other items authenticated by the other criteria. Is that obviously a stupid proposal?

As it turns out, however, the criteria are only occasionally up to the job they were designed to do—so much so that we must deem them to be promises without fulfillment. They have brought no more consensus to our discipline than would otherwise have existed without them; and different scholars have used the very same criteria to obtain very different ends. The reason is that tools do not dictate how they are used; the hands that hold them do that. You can use screwdrivers to remove screws, and you can use screwdrivers to install screws. And so it is with dissimilarity, multiple attestation, embarrassment, and coherence. The pliable nature of these criteria is such that critical scholars can do and have done just about anything with them. The evidence for this conclusion I cannot offer here.[5] I do note, however, that the number of scholars dissatisfied with the standard criteria of authenticity seems to have increased significantly of late. Several of us have tossed them aside for good and are now trying other things.[6]

The deficiencies of the standard criteria are not the only problem for Funk. There is also the issue of how much material he has to subtract to get his Jesus. It is one thing to excise this or that saying because it fails to resonate with the rest of the tradition. It is quite another to remove dozens and dozens of sayings in a variety of genres and from every source and stratum of the tradition, as does Funk. He indeed regards the majority of sayings and events in the gospels as being apocryphal. Does this result not defeat his method?

It is in theory conceivable that Jesus uttered a very high percentage of the sayings the Synoptics impute to him. In such a case, we obviously would know a good deal about him and might even be able to sort out some of the secondary additions. Yet it is also in theory conceivable that Jesus authored, let us say, only six of those sayings. In this alternative scenario, the tradition would be so thoroughly corrupt that our knowledge about him would be minimal and in fact insufficient for us to figure out which six sayings it was that he did utter. Sometimes we can scrape off corrosion and get to the metal. Other times the corrosion is such that the metal is no longer there.

Now I am unsure exactly where, between the first hypothetical situation—a high percentage of the tradition goes back to Jesus—and the second—only six sayings go back to him—is the line at which our sources

---

5. For this see Dale C. Allison, Jr., "How to Marginalize the Criteria of Authenticity," in *The Handbook of the Study of the Historical Jesus*, ed. Tom Holmen and Stanley E. Porter, 4 vols. (Leiden: Brill, 2010) 1:3–30.

6. For my own attempt, see *Constructing Jesus* (Grand Rapids: Baker Academic, 2010).

become sufficiently unreliable so as to put the quest beyond our ability. But I am pretty sure that Funk has crossed it. His excision of so much material means we have too much false testimony. His task becomes like trying to solve a criminal case without a reliable witness: it is all but impossible. Surely the sources for the Jesus tradition must give us enough decent memory to work with or we are out of luck; that is, they need to tell the truth often enough for us to figure out when they might not be telling the truth.

I should add that this is a purely historical argument, not Christian apologetics. If we cannot credibly come up with a Jesus too far from the synoptic portrait, that is only because we have no competing sources. Paul tells us a few things about Jesus, but not a whole lot, and he does not contradict the Synoptics in any significant way. The extracanonical gospels, such as the Gospel of Thomas, do not really change the picture, nor does John's Gospel, although that is a topic for another day.

We can imagine it being otherwise. Although I have read documents published by the Church of Jesus Christ of Latter Day Saints, their picture of Joseph Smith is not my picture. The reason is that I have also studied documents containing accounts from non-Mormons and ex-Mormons who knew Joseph Smith, and I have come to conclusions that ill suit the official Mormon narratives. But if all I had were the official texts, if I had no competing materials, I could not have constructed my alternative story. I would, for various reasons, have a certain prejudice against many of the relevant claims, but I would not have any real data with which to essay a rival account. I would be stuck with choosing between something closely related to the official story and no story at all, that is, skepticism.

It is the same with the Synoptics. If we had the diaries of Jesus, or the diaries of his brother James, or the diaries of Peter, then we might feel confident going against the canonical consensus in major ways. We might even be forced to excise large swaths of material as legendary or to discount the larger impressions the gospels leave us with. We do not, however, have such competing materials. So we are pretty much stuck with playing variations on the Jesus we have in our canonical texts—or, if we refuse to do that, with doing nothing. The restricted nature of what has survived does not allow us to stray too far from the synoptic Jesus, even though Funk and so many others have made the attempt.

I have yet another objection to Funk's procedure of subtraction and reconfiguration. Human memories are, as modern cognitive science has demonstrated, constantly evolving generalizations. We tend to retain "whole events, whole faces, whole conversations, not the sub-plots, the features, the words that make them up."[7] And as our memories move from short-term to long-term storage, they are disposed to retain, if anything, only the substance or gist of an event. We may forget the words and syntax of a sentence yet still remember its general substance or meaning. We construct memories of people and events in the same way we reproduce maps from our heads: we omit most of the details, straighten the lines, and round off the angles, thereby creating a sort of minimalist cartoon.

Given that memory is fuzzy, that we remember the outlines of an event or the general import of a conversation better than the details, that we extract patterns and meaning from informational input, it would be peculiar to imagine that, although their general impressions of him were hopelessly skewed, early Christian tradents somehow managed to recall, with some accuracy, a couple of dozen parables of Jesus and a handful of his one-liners. For the same reason, it would be peculiar to imagine that we can reconstruct Jesus, as does Funk, by hunting for some incidents and sayings that pass through the gauntlet of our authenticating criteria while setting aside the general impressions our primary sources instill in us.

What we know of memory moves me to dissent from scholars who proceed by subtraction and presume that we can learn about Jesus chiefly on the basis of the relatively few items that are deemed, after critical sorting and repeated subtraction, to be authentic. The larger the generalization and the more data upon which it is based, the greater our confidence. The more specific the detail and the fewer the supporting data, the greater our uncertainty. So, in the matter of Jesus, we should start not with the parts but with the whole, by which I mean we should heed first the general impressions that the tradition about him, *in toto*, tends to convey. For that is where the best memories are likely to reside. Funk has things backwards. But then that is the only way he or anybody can fashion a Jesus truly dissimilar from the figure in the Synoptics.

With that, let me turn aside from Funk and from attempts to recover a Jesus significantly dissimilar from what we find in the Synoptics and consider instead the very different attempts to defend everything we find there. For if there have been and continue to be academics who seek to configure a substantially new Jesus, there likewise have been and continue to be scholars whose antithetical goal is to prove that the canonical texts are rock-solid history through and through, that Jesus uttered everything

---

7. John Henderson, *Memory and Forgetting* (London: Routledge, 1999) 28–29.

the New Testament attributes to him, and that he did everything the New Testament recounts him as doing. My contention—this is my second large generalization—is that the more conservative aspiration is as futile as the more liberal aspiration, for it too seeks to do the impossible.

Many Christian apologists have, over the centuries, felt a need to establish the historicity of the gospels. They have tried several strategies. They have urged, for example, that the correlations between the gospels and Old Testament prophecies establish the trustworthiness of the gospels. Defenders of the faith have also argued that the traditional ascriptions to Matthew, Mark, Luke, and John are correct, which means that at least two of our authors—Matthew and John—were eyewitnesses, and that another—Mark—was a friend of Peter, yet a third eyewitness. Another popular tactic for upholding the mnemonic accuracy of the gospels has been to harmonize them, to iron out all the differences, to show that, despite frequent appearances, their testimony is invariably unified.

These traditional strategies have fallen on hard times. The deists assaulted the proof from prophecy, showing that it is not so hard to correlate recent events with old poetic oracles; and, more recently, study of the Dead Sea Scrolls has reinforced their case, for now we have non-Christian texts from the turn of the era that also claim to espy the realization of Old Testament prophecies in the experience of a Jewish religious group. One understands why most modern theologians regard the proof from prophecy as no longer possessing evidentiary force.

Harmonization of the gospels is also no longer in vogue. David Fredrich Strauss, in the middle of the nineteenth century, demonstrated once and for all the feebleness of the enterprise.[8] Arguing that the variations between Matthew 4 and Luke 4 require that the devil tempted Jesus on two very similar but different occasions is just plain silly; and when Mark 15:12 tells us that "it was nine o'clock in the morning when they crucified" Jesus, whereas John 19:14–16 reports that "it was about noon" when "they handed him over to be crucified," there is no credible reconciliation. There are real differences between the gospels. As Origen, Calvin, Maldonatus, and a few other premodern yet astute exegetes rightly recognized, the canonical witnesses do not agree on everything that Jesus said, nor do they concur on everything that happened to him.[9]

---

8. David Friedrich Strauss, *The Life of Jesus Critically Examined* (Philadelphia: Fortress, 1972).

9. For the relevant passages from Origen, Calvin, and Maldonatus, see my *Historical Christ and the Theological Jesus* (Grand Rapids: Eerdmans, 2009) 1–2.

What of the appeal to eyewitnesses? The problems here are manifold. Very few specialists any longer suppose that Matthew was written by Matthew or John by John; and even if John Mark, the friend of Peter, composed the Second Gospel, how could we determine what derives directly from the apostle and what derives from other sources?

Beyond that, eyewitnesses can do things other than remember. Plato was a companion of Socrates, but most of what the student puts in the mouth of his teacher was not said by him. And what of Marco Polo, who claims to have seen all sorts of things that he could not have seen, such as a bird that could lift an elephant? Or King George IV, who remembered leading his troops at Waterloo, although he was nowhere near the battle?

Personal reminiscence is neither innocent nor objective. Observers habitually misremember as much as they misperceive. Memory mixes together like events; it gets contaminated by post-event information; it dramatizes; it assimilates to social expectation; it reads present beliefs into the past; it reorders events; it revises to serve contemporary goals; it sculpts recall according to narrative conventions. Thucydides saw the basic truth ages ago: "Different eyewitnesses give different accounts of the same events, speaking out of partiality for one side or the other or else from imperfect memories."[10]

So what is to be done? Let me introduce you to another historian, whose ways are not Funk's ways. Craig Blomberg is a distinguished professor of New Testament at Denver Seminary, an evangelical institution. His book *The Historical Reliability of the Gospels* is an attempt to prove the title's truth: the gospels are, in all essentials, historically reliable.[11] Ironically, he can make use of the very same tools that Funk uses—dissimilarity, multiple attestation, embarrassment, coherence. Blomberg's conclusions, however, are antithetical to those of Funk.

Blomberg avows that "patient application of the criteria of authenticity can itself eventually lead one to accept virtually all of the Gospel tradition."[12] For him, those tools can establish that Jesus was tempted in the wilderness, that he was transfigured into light, that he repeatedly predicted his own resurrection, that he spoke of his own divine origin, and so on.

---

10. Thucydides, *History of the Peloponnesian War* 1.22.

11. Craig Blomberg, *The Historical Reliability of the Gospels*, 2nd ed. (Downers Grove, IL: IVP Academic, 2007).

12. Ibid., 318.

My problem with Blomberg is the same as my problem with Funk. The criteria of authenticity are not the magical keys to the past: they cannot prove so much. The gap between what has happened and what we can discover or prove to have happened is much larger than we care to imagine. That something took place scarcely entails our ability to show that it took place. Blomberg's historical reach too often exceeds his historical grasp.

My experience is altogether different from those who, whether conservative or skeptical or something else, wield the criteria to come to definite conclusions. Time and time again I have looked at a saying and weighed the arguments on both sides—and there are always arguments pro and con, usually good arguments pro and con—and been unable to come up with more than this: Well, Jesus may very well have said this or something very much like it; certainly no one has shown that he did not; but all the arguments concocted to establish that he in fact did fall short. In like manner I have often thought: Well, I see no reason to doubt that such an event took place, yet how could we ever muster the proof that it did? Origen was more astute than many modern historians when he observed long ago: "The endeavor to show, with regard to almost any history, however true, that it actually occurred . . . is one of the most difficult undertakings that can be attempted, and is in some instances an impossibility."[13]

Let me hasten to add that I am a skeptic only from one point of view. Acknowledging our inability to prove that something happened is not at all the same as concluding that it did not happen. I am not offering a skeptical analysis of the historical content of the gospels—I think, on the contrary, that they tell us a lot about Jesus—but a skeptical analysis about our ability, as historians, following the rules of the historian's guild, to determine precisely that content. Furthermore, and despite all that I have said, I do believe that historians can construct some respectable arguments for the authenticity of certain items in the tradition. We can, for instance, make a decent case that Jesus prohibited divorce and that he threatened the destruction of Jerusalem's temple; we can come up with some good reasons for holding that twelve of his disciples formed a special group and that one of them betrayed him; and we can establish beyond doubt that he was crucified and even, I believe, show the likelihood that he was buried by someone named Joseph of Arimathea.

The problem, and why the conservative project fails just like the liberal project, is that most of the traditions do not allow us to get hold of them in

---

13. Origen, *Contra Celsus* 1.42.

this manner. How could one ever prove that Jesus in fact uttered some version of the golden rule (Matt 7:12 = Luke 6:31), which has so many parallels in worldwide wisdom? How could we establish, with reasonable conviction, that he implored, "Do not let the left hand know what the right hand is doing," an imperative solely attested in a Gospel—Matthew—written fifty or more years after his death (6:3)? How could we mount a case that he really healed a blind man named Bartimaeus, for which our only real source is Mark (10:46–52)? How could we come up with strong evidence that, at some spot in the Palestinian wilderness, Jesus fed a large crowd of people with minimal provisions, even if all four gospels purport that he did (Matt 14:13–21; Mark 6:32–44; Luke 9:10–17; John 6:1–15)? How could we demonstrate that a herd of pigs once ran over a cliff in response to something Jesus said (Mark 5:1–20)? Even were the archaeologists to dig up some pig bones near the right spot, what would that prove, in the strong sense of the word? Maybe the story was invented to explain a bone pile. Of course, it is equally true that no one could ever show that some pigs did not turn into lemmings when Jesus appeared on the scene.

Let me emphasize that I have come to my conclusions about the limitations of historians, which means my own limitations, only after a long struggle. If I had begun as the partial cynic that I have become, it's possible I would have tried another vocation because, in my youth, my aspiration really was to determine what really happened. Anyway, I was taught in graduate school to employ the criteria of authenticity, and for years I obediently did what my professors told me to do. Eventually, however, the truth began to peek around the corner—the truth that, most often, the criteria are of little help, and that the pile of materials that we can confidently demonstrate to be historical is much smaller than the pile that we cannot so judge.

My own view, after years of work in this field, is that too many people have expected too much from us historians of Jesus, and that we ourselves have suffered from a Sherlock Holmes complex, imagining that we can ascertain, with a degree of assurance that would convince an open-minded jury, the origin of every item in the tradition. Sadly, it is not so. Only sometimes can we give compelling reasons for thinking that Jesus said or did not say exactly this, or did or did not do exactly that. Historians are not omnipotent; we cannot do everything.

So much, then, for my negations, for what historians cannot do. What is it that we can do? Are we good for anything? Perhaps. Let me offer two more large generalizations for your consideration. The first is this. If we are frustrated by our ability to establish the origin of so many individual items in the tradition, our knowledge of the historical Jesus is, on purely historical grounds, nonetheless considerable. This is because the first-century traditions associated with his name are not an amorphous mess. On the contrary, certain themes, motifs, and rhetorical strategies recur again and again throughout the primary sources; and we may reasonably hold that, in those themes and motifs and rhetorical strategies—which, taken together, leave some distinct impressions—we find good memory.

To illustrate: the traditions about Jesus have him referring often to the kingdom of God, from which I infer, even if I cannot authenticate any particular saying, that he had much to say about that kingdom. I draw similar inferences from the many sayings that have him speaking about future reward, about future judgment, about suffering for the saints, about victory over evil powers, about the importance of intention, about the loving fatherhood of God, about the dangers of wealth, about the demand to love the marginal and those unlike oneself, and any number of other recurrent themes. The repeated thematic patterns must give us the historical Jesus if anything does. So too the formal literary features, or what may be called rhetorical strategies, that appear again and again. Thus we may safely infer, from the wide attestation across the sources, that Jesus spoke in parables, that he liked rhetorical questions, that he used prefatory "amen," that he was fond of hyperbole, that he was given to formulating aphorisms, and so on.

Anyone who doubts these things should distrust the tradition as a whole and find something else to fret about. Certain themes, motifs, and rhetorical strategies are sufficiently well attested that we face an inevitable choice. Either those themes, motifs, and rhetorical strategies tend to preserve pre-Easter memories or they do not. If, as we have reason to think,[14] they do preserve such memories, we have a lot to ponder. We might not be able to establish beyond reasonable doubt that Jesus must have composed this saying or performed precisely that act; yet we can, taking the tradition in its entirety, know the sorts of things that he was wont to say and the sorts of things that he was wont to do. Indeed, I believe that we even know much about his character and his intentions.

If, however, one doubts that the recurrent themes and motifs and rhetorical strategies fairly represent what Jesus was all about, then the tradition is misleading in its broad features and the game is over. If our sources do

---

14. See further Allison, *Constructing Jesus*, passim.

not remember well, we cannot remember for them. Nor can we, if they are so close to amnesia, somehow fish out the handful of genuine memories from amid all the fiction. So again I stress that attempts to find a historical Jesus too much unlike the synoptic figure are futile. If the answer to the question, "Where is Jesus?" turns out to be like the answer to the question, "Where's Waldo?"—namely, in only one tiny spot on every page—the quest is vain. If, however, as we have reason to believe, Jesus is much more present than that, we are open for business.

So much for my third large generality. My fourth and final generalization takes me back to Schweitzer. We remember him for his entertaining history of the quest. But we also remember him for his portrait of Jesus as an eschatological prophet. According to Schweitzer, Jesus had a thoroughly eschatological worldview. When he called for repentance because the kingdom of God was at hand, he meant that the end was near. When he said that "this generation will not pass away before all these things take place," he meant that the end was near. And when he told his disciples that the Son of Man would return before they had finished going through the cities of Israel, he meant that the end was near. Jesus construed his present and near future as the great tribulation before the grand consummation; and he understood his own role in properly messianic terms.

Schweitzer characterized his approach, which offended so many, as "thorough-going eschatology." Although the phrase claims too much, he was nonetheless on to something. He may have gotten many of the details wrong, but he was, in what I take to be the main point, surely right. The Jesus of history, if the Synoptics are any guide, was not solely about ethics, and for him the kingdom was not social progress. He rather had a stupendous self-conception—a messianic self-conception—and, beyond that, he was captivated by eschatology.[15] This is why we hear him speak so often of "the (day of) judgment," which by his time had become a synonym for the eschatological trial that will reward the righteous and punish the wicked. And this is why he refers on multiple occasions to "Gehenna," which became, in the intertestamental period, the name for the antithesis of heaven, the frightful place of postmortem or end-time punishment. And this is why he likens the present crisis to Noah's flood and Sodom's demise, both of those primeval calamities being, in the Jewish and Christian lore of his time, popular prototypes of the last judgment and end of the present age (Luke 17:26–30; cf. Matt 24:37–39). And on and on it goes. Jesus

---

15. In addition to what follows, see my *Constructing Jesus*, 31–164.

recurrently gains God's perspective on the present by placing himself in the future and looking back.

Eschatology is the key to a whole host of sayings. When Jesus solemnly declares that the first will be last, the last first (Matt 10:39 = Luke 17:33; Matt 23:12 = Luke 14:11; etc.), he is not being naively optimistic about everyday human experience, which too often sees the rich get richer, the poor poorer. He instead uses the future tense because this is prophecy: God will turn the world upside down in the coming judgment. When Jesus tells us to pray, "your kingdom come" (Matt 6:10 = Luke 11:2), the liturgical parallels in Judaism make it clear enough that he is thinking of the resurrection and the judgment. When Jesus exhorts people to enter the kingdom of God, he is counseling them to do whatever it takes to enter into life, which means the eternal life of the age to come (Mark 10:15, 23–25; Matt 5:20; 7:13–14, 21; 23:13). And when Jesus blesses the hungry and those who weep because they will be filled and laugh (Matt 5:4, 6 = Luke 21), he is being deliberately unrealistic, for he is anticipating a world miraculously made new; he is consoling those unable to find consolation until the world ceases to be what it is now.

Jesus believed that, although God had created a good world, evil spirits have filled it with wickedness, so that it is in disarray and full of injustice. He believed that a day is coming when God will repair the broken creation and restore scattered Israel. He believed that, before that time, the struggle between good and evil will come to a climax, and a period of great tribulation and unmatched woe will descend upon the world. And he believed that, after this period, God will reward the just and the unjust, both living and dead, and then, through Jesus himself, establish divine rule forever.

For me, sober recognition of Jesus' eschatological orientation is perhaps the chief accomplishment, if it has any, of the quest for the historical Jesus. Whatever else he may have been, Jesus was, as Schweitzer insisted, an eschatological prophet. The quest has also taught us, through its attention to ancient Jewish apocalyptic literature, that his brand of eschatology should be construed in terms that his contemporaries would have understood. This means acknowledging the importance of ancient Jewish apocalyptic literature for understanding Jesus, and likewise paying close attention to rabbinic sources, because Jesus' words about the "kingdom of God" have so many close parallels in what the rabbis say regarding the ʻolam habbah, the world to come.[16]

---

16. See further ibid., 164–204.

At this point, however, I wish to step out of my role as historian and speak, for a few minutes, as I wind down, in personal, religious terms.

Although the eschatological Jesus troubles many Christians, he does not trouble me. The reason is that I hate much of this world that God made, and I crave the sort of transcendent resolution and happy ending that Jesus repeatedly envisages. If the Holocaust was the eternal termination of consciousness for its victims, and there is nothing more, then I doubt that God is good in any relevant sense; and if leukemia takes little Susie when she is eight years old, and there is no future of any kind for her, then I do not believe that God is love. If the sufferings of the present time are never undone, then I concede the field to atheism.

But I am not an atheist because I hope that the present things will pass away, that someday and somehow the providence of God will see to it that mourning and crying and pain will be no more. I share the dream that Dostoevsky put into the mouth of Ivan Karamazov, which I take to be the dream of Jesus:

> I trust that the wounds will heal, the scars will vanish, that the sorry and ridiculous spectacle of humanity's disagreements and clashes will disappear like a pitiful mirage, like the sordid invention of a puny, microscopic, Euclidean, human brain, and that, in the end, in the universal finale, at the moment universal harmony is achieved, something so magnificent will take place that it will satisfy every human heart, allay all indignation, pay for all human crimes, for all the blood shed by people, and enable everyone not only to forgive everything but also to justify everything that has happened to human beings.[17]

Of course no one can fathom how such a thing might be done. It is impossible, unimaginable. But precisely in doing the unimaginable and the impossible, God will prove to be God.

I find myself in this matter also drawn to some words, less dramatic but still forceful, of an older British New Testament scholar, B. H. Streeter, who responded to what Schweitzer had wrought with these words:

> The summits of certain mountains are seen only at rare moments when, their cloud-cap rolled away, they stand out stark and clear. So in ordinary life ultimate values and eternal issues are normally obscured by minor duties, petty cares, and small ambitions; at the bedside of a dying man the cloud is often lifted. In virtue of the

---

17. Fyodor Dostoevsky, *The Brothers Karamazov* (New York: Bantam, 1970) 283.

> eschatological hope our Lord and His first disciples found themselves standing, as it were, at the bedside of a dying world. Thus for a whole generation the cloud of lesser interests was rolled away, and ultimate values and eternal issues stood out before them stark and clear.... The majority of men in all ages best serve their kind by a life of quiet duty, in the family, in their daily work, and in the support of certain definite and limited public and philanthropic causes.... But it has been well for humanity that during one great epoch the belief that the end of all was near turned the thoughts of the highest minds away from practical and local interests, even of the first importance, like the condition of slaves in Capernaum or the sanitation of Tarsus.[18]

As these words make excellent sense to me, I find the eschatological Jesus more than congenial—and congenial even if he hoped that the end was near, as Schweitzer scandalously urged. I would, although the theologians might object, put his sense of imminence down to his authentic humanity and then ask, quite seriously: If one truly believes that God is in love with the whole world, passionately and wholeheartedly in love with the whole world and with everyone in it, how can one not hope or even believe that the divinity will, in the very next minute, call a halt to the tortured experiment that history has become? How can our loving God, who does not give us a stone when we ask for bread and who registers even the fall of the sparrow, endure any longer the sort of suffering that overflows the four corners of this world each and every day—gratuitous suffering on a massive, unthinkable scale? I continually wonder why God does not scream and stop it all now.

Whatever the resolution, I detest much of this world that Genesis declares, against so much of the evidence, to be good. My list of complaints is very long. I despise brain cancer, which devoured my father's mind. I abhor the Civil War, whose battlefields do not enthuse me but make me sick at heart. I hate the sight of dead animals beside our indifferent highways, their shattered carcasses being for me questions about the nature of our callous world.

Above all, I hate the everlasting victory of death. It is not just the innate fear of the unknown or of annihilation. Nor is it only the miserable

---

18. B. H. Streeter, "The Historic Christ," in Streeter et al., *Foundations: A Statement of Christian Belief in Terms of Modern Thought: By Seven Oxford Men* (London: Macmillan, 1913) 119–20.

heartbreak of interminable separation, although that is beyond intolerable: they go; they all go; and they never come back.

Beyond all that, I hate the boredom of mortality. We are born. We live. And then we die. And it is always so. It never changes. How can a game whose ending is always the same hold any interest? Death makes everything unspeakably boring. All we can do is eat and drink, for tomorrow we die.

But then there is Jesus, the eschatological visionary. He imagines and proclaims a better world than this one, where the gates of Hades will no longer prevail. He prays for God's will to descend so that things become on earth as they are in heaven. He comforts those who mourn, because there will be neither mourning nor crying nor pain anymore, when the former things pass away. However one works out the interpretive details, it is perfectly clear that Jesus, in the theological idiom of the first century, teaches and lives an extravagant hope, expecting and avowing that tragedy and death are not the final chapters.

That is why his words so often speak of judgment, resurrection, and the kingdom of God. He has an audacious vision, which is ruled above all else by the conviction that God the Father is good. Jesus' theology demands that there be something more, something better, something far better. The divine future must remake and redeem the wreck that history has become. It must, Jesus says again and again in different similes, turn this cosmic tragedy into a universal comedy.

I hope to God that Jesus was right.

My hope not only clings to his words. For Jesus is more than a talking head, and although he has a story to tell, he also has a story to live. And that story, as the New Testament relates it, incarnates his speech.

Recall with me the last few verses of Mark (16:1–8). The sun, prematurely dark the day before, begins to lighten the horizon. We see Mary Magdalene and two or three other women. It is less than a full day since the crucifixion, death, and burial of their dear friend, and they are walking with heads down. The road is dusty, and their hearts are broken. Their feet are dirty, and there is no life in their dragging steps. They are in shock; their words are few. There are little tracks on their cheeks, made by their tears; and they are walking to a silent grave, where they will wail and weep again.

They know what they are going to find, because death, in its eternal victory, mistreats all its victims the same way. They are going to touch cold flesh. They are going to speak to deaf ears. They are going to see rigid limbs. And they are going to breathe in an unpleasant odor.

When they finally arrive, however, the utterly unexpected overtakes them. Not a corpse, but an angel. Not silence, but a proclamation: "He has been raised. He is not here. Look, there is the place they laid him." And with that, what Jesus envisaged has come to life in his own experience. He has become the exception that breaks the rule, the rule of death. And all of a sudden, the game, for everybody, ceases to be boring.

Or so that is how I think about it. The historical Jesus is the eschatological Jesus, whose words display the fundamental pattern of Jewish apocalyptic, which is unprecedented human suffering succeeded by everlasting divine vindication. His story is that pattern. For his death and resurrection are the end of the world in miniature, and God's exaltation of Jesus is the vindication of his eschatological imagination.

3

Why the Roman Cross?

Katherine Sonderegger

As a young man, but already a fighter, Athanasius took up with classic virtuosity and directness the question that lies before us today: Why the cross? Why did Jesus Christ have to die on a Roman cross "for us and for our salvation"? In his great early treatise, *On the Incarnation of the Word*, Athanasius grasps firmly the deep mystery of Christ's manner of death: "If any of our people," he writes, "inquire, not from love of debate,"—he, the great debater!—"but from love of learning, why Christ suffered death in none other way save on the Cross, let him also be told that no other way than this was good for us, and that it was well that the Lord suffered this for our sakes."[1] Athanasius does not let the matter rest there, however. He dares to spell out in just what way the cross was "good for us," and "well" that Jesus Christ "suffered for our sakes"—a phrase already redolent of the Nicene Creed that would soon emerge from Athanasius' vigorous battle against the Arians.

Now I should be quick to say, before I follow his doctrine here, that Athanasius' reputation has suffered some rough treatment at the hands of modern historians. It has not always been so. The prominent Victorian editor Archibald Robertson could stoutly defend Athanasius as a "commanding personality"—even more, as "a saint" and a "Christian hero"—and roundly

---

1. *De Incarnatione*, §25.1, trans. Archibald Robertson.

conclude, "Secular as well as Church historians fall under the spell of his personality, and even Gibbon lays aside his 'solemn sneer' to do homage to Athanasius the great."[2] But the "cloud of romance" these eminent Victorians could see surrounding Athanasius has long since fallen away. Modern historians of ancient Christianity—R. C. Hanson and Lewis Ayres are good examples—find Athanasius' character a full measure short of "greatness" and "heroism" and advance the once heretical suggestion that the treatise we have open before us, *On the Incarnation*, was hardly influential and well known in its own day, and, even more, is known in ours only because of its ardent, and misguided, admirers in the English universities of the nineteenth century. Now, we need not settle such scholarly debates here; but we might bear in mind, as we reflect on this essay, and the doctrine set before us, that the ambiguity of history touches even the greatest of theologians and their theology, and that the gracious light of the cross must fall on the Christian saint and hero—perhaps especially on them—just as it must on the everyday, unvarnished sinner and scholar who comes afterward and rests on that ancient work.

To return now to Athanasius. In a short and remarkable chapter, Athanasius lays out a rich and expansive justification for the cross of Jesus Christ. He begins with the Apostle Paul: "How else," he argues, "could Christ have 'become a curse' unless he received the death set for a curse? and that is the Cross." Then Athanasius evokes the cross as "ransom," though to a different end than we have been taught to view the "ransom account of the atonement": "How would Christ have called all nations to him, had he not been crucified? For it is only on the cross that a man dies with his hands spread out." In a lovely image that recalls in our day the famous "two hands" of Irenaeus' God the Father (the Son and the Holy Spirit), Athanasius continues: "It was fitting for the Lord to spread out his hands, that with the one he might draw the ancient people"—that is, the covenant people, Israel—"and with the other those from the Gentiles, and unite both in himself." He concludes his list with a startling cosmological image of the kind that delighted the church fathers: Christ is "lifted up" on the cross and in the way that is both "perfect" and "fitting," "he cleared the air of the malignity both of the devil and of demons of all kinds, and made a new opening of the way into heaven." All this is a substitution for, and an assumption of, our plight: "For

---

2. *Nicene and Post-Nicene Fathers*, 4:lxvii, lxviii.

as Christ offered his own body to death on behalf of all, so by it he once more made ready the way up into the heavens."³

So, I might express Athanasius' doctrine of the cross of Christ in this shorthand and modern idiom: Christ's death by crucifixion takes on the curse of sin and rebellion against God, enacts and symbolizes the union of Jew and Gentile, and purges the cosmos of demonic evil, opening the transcendent freedom of God to the entire world. I find Athanasius' doctrine of the cross compelling, rich, and deeply mysterious; I invite you to consider with me how we might follow his lead in our own confessions today of the saving death of Christ on the cross.

Let me begin with an area that has quite properly received a good deal of attention in present-day theologies of atonement: "the union of Jew and Gentile" in the passion and cross of Christ. Now, it is not easy in our season of Christian theology, a season most soberly and fittingly stamped by the horror and shame of the Shoah (or Holocaust), to express Athanasius' point with proper nuance and power. I will hazard an interpretation: Why must Jesus Christ die on a *Roman* cross? I want to underscore something, then, that our ancestors in the faith did not feel or perceive as their theological obligation: that the instrument of Christ's death was a specifically Roman form of execution, one that sums up with a particular, and searing, form of ferocity the relation between Israel and the Gentiles, between Israel and the reigning "great powers" of the day.

Like any ancient empire—like any modern nation-state, we might add—Rome had devised a means of capital punishment that could be used as a threat and executed upon the criminals in its midst. Now there are two elements to this savage form of state execution that mark it off, I would say, from its modern equivalents. Crucifixion by its very design, and not by some cruel accident, inflicted torment on its victims. Other forms of state execution, even the most heinous of modern state killings, such as gas chambers or killing squads, are designed to be *efficient*—a quick death, invisible, if possible, to the tender consciences of the executioners. Not so the cross!

We who have witnessed the renewed respectability of torture—coolly sanitized as the "torture debate"—should have fixed in our minds, I believe, just what a death by torture entails. The death of Jesus sears these brutalities into our minds and our very viscera. The enemy of the state is held in a dark prison, little more than a pit, where the contempt and shaming of

---

3. *De Incarnatione*, §25.2–6.

the victim can begin, unseen and unchecked. The Apostle Paul has many reason for calling the cross "shameful"—we will examine more of them in a moment—but one must surely be this: in the whole, sustained act of bringing a criminal to the cross, a human being, a living creature of God, becomes an *object*, a thing and a plaything of great powers, which humiliate and mock a human self into a parody of a human form. This *object* of ridicule—we can take the terms in full earnestness here—is then beaten and whipped; the biblical term for this is "flogged," and the Romans often used iron bars for this cruelty, a fact Paul knew full well. The point of these torments, as with many modern forms of torture, is to allow the victim to *live*. Death is the release, not the penalty, for any subject of torture.

Crucifixion itself is a Roman execution that distilled these many torments. Here the shadow of a man was suspended from a crossbeam, hung by his own flesh, on a pole stuck into the blood-soaked earth. The victim is exposed in every way. Stripped, bleeding and raw, naked to the avid gaze of spectators, exposed to taunting and contempt, the crucified slowly died of their own weight, starving for breath, for water, and for pity. We have an idea, though only an imperfect one, and by distance, of this cruel practice when we examine the terrible picture of American lynchings—public executions of great cruelty and shame attended by white crowds who considered the hangings both a terror and a deep, dehumanizing pleasure. The breaking of the leg bones—in itself a cruel savagery—was, for the crucified, a mercy: they would be quickly hanged by their own unsupported bodies. We recall from Scripture that Jesus was not subjected to such cruel mercy—not a bone of his body was broken—but this is because he died quickly—only three hours. Some victims of this Roman torment survived for *days* in this unspeakable state. Crucifixion, like almost all tortures, is designed to terrify and control the peoples who witness it. The cross was remarkably effective. And we can see why the cross was feared by every subject people of the empire. And on this Roman tree of cruelty hung the Son of Man for the deliverance of the world.

Now, the Roman cross differs from modern-day forms of execution in a second way as well. Unlike modern capital punishments carried out by the nation-state, the Roman practice of crucifixion was reserved for a *specific* population. The cross was the brutal death designated for subject peoples—foreigners and non-Romans—and for slaves. The Apostle Paul's Roman citizenship was prized exactly for this reason: it brought one into the courts of law, not the prison chamber, and permitted an efficient form of death—by sword, perhaps, or beheading. We can see this kind of discrimination in the Tudor monarchy, for example. Royals and royal favorites are allowed to die by beheading—the solemn baring of a monarch's neck to the executioner was actually a mercy—while the rest were tortured by a slow, cruel burning, or more shocking still, by being broken apart by straining teams of powerful animals—being "drawn and quartered." The cross of Christ, then, was a death for slaves and exiles, an imperial execution for those under the lordship of the Caesar, but without the protection of citizenship. It was the death of an alien and immigrant, a criminal, a rebel and a slave.

Now it is just these elements of the cross of Christ—its particular savagery as a Roman execution for slaves—that the Gospel of John brings to the fore. Modern critics have frequently faulted, and with great cogency exposed, the anti-Judaism of the Gospel of John. We catch a flavor of this polemic against the covenant people in the Fourth Evangelist's frequent use of the phrase "the Jews," a category seldom favorable in the text. I do not want to dismiss so serious a charge against this Gospel, but I do here want to examine another layer, this time much more positive and complex, of this Gospel when it treats the death of Jesus on a Roman cross. Two elements command our attention: the death of Jesus is expressly and deliberately tied to Rome and the Roman imperium; and the death is tied, again expressly and deliberatively, to the high festival of Passover.

You remember the exchange between the Jewish leadership and their guards, and Pontius Pilate, the Roman procurator of Judea. Pilate moves out of his palace to meet the delegation from Caiaphas: "What accusation do you bring?" Their answer, a condemnation and a discharge of responsibility: "If he were not a malefactor, we would not have delivered him up to you." Pilate is equal to such a thrust; a savvy and ruthless governor, Pilate can parry away an unwanted burden: "Take him and judge him according to *your* law." "The Jews"—John's use is deliberate here—said in turn: "It is not lawful for us to put any man to death." The Evangelist interprets this verse for us: This was to fulfill the saying of Jesus which signified what kind of death he should die.[4] Increasingly, the drama narrows down to an exchange between Jesus and Pilate, a mismatched struggle over kingship. Pilate enthrones himself on the judgement seat, and this scene of execution is given both Greek and Hebrew—that is, Aramaic—names so that we will hear once again that this is a trial between Judea and Rome, Jew

---

4. John 18:30–32.

and Gentile. "And it was the preparation for the Passover" John solemnly reminds us, when Pilate sat down as a little Caesar over his restless subjects. So that we cannot forget the political nature of this combat, Pilate restates his mocking judgment: "Behold your king!" he tells "the Jews." "Shall I crucify your king?" Pilate again taunts. The chief priests answer with chilling realism: "We have no king but Caesar."[5] Now, what shall we say about such an exchange?

Unmistakable is the emphasis upon the *Roman* cross: it could be no other because Jews no longer possessed the right of capital punishment—"It is not lawful for us to put any man to death." We have here a classic summary of statecraft: a nation that has become a colony or client state no longer holds the ultimate power over its subjects. Its status as a dependent and conquered nation is underscored and made concrete by its inability to execute its criminals. Just as colonial states have no power to enact separate treaties or to wage war, so a client state or colony cannot determine the life and death of its population. The emperor alone controls life and death in the empire and its possessions. Just this the ruling party in Judea acknowledges and confirms: "We have no king but Caesar." As Messiah, as king, Jesus will not be executed by his own people. This death is not a regicide like the execution of Charles I, nor slaughter on the battlefield, like King Saul, nor death to a rebel son like Absalom; Christ's death is rather the execution by the imperial government of a royal claimant through a death reserved for an alien, a troublesome colonial, and an offscouring, a slave. Jesus is not accorded the death of a heretic or martyr, like Stephen, or threatened with the death of a sexual offender, like the woman caught in adultery; Jesus is not stoned, nor does he expect to be, John tells us. He will rather be raised up from the earth on the cross, crucified in this particular imperial torment, as king who rivaled Caesar.

Nor is this death and manner of death opposed to the other Johannine, indeed Gospel, affirmation, that Christ's death was an event of the Passover. It has been traditional in the liturgical rehearsal of the great record of our salvation to link Passover directly with the history of the covenant, the history of God's mighty acts of deliverance to the people Israel. Certainly, this is both fitting and profound. But it has the unanticipated effect, I believe, of joining the death of Jesus *directly* and *explicitly* with Israel and with first-century Jews, as if Jesus were killed by his own people as they readied for escape from an empire. So too does the assimilation of the

5. John 19:13–16.

Passover slaughter to Temple sacrifice locate Jesus' execution as a Jewish cultic death, an assimilation firmly declared by von Balthasar in his great *Mysterium Paschale*.[6] There are, to be sure, important elements of sacrifice in the death of Christ! One could scarcely glance at the letters of Paul, or the Passion predictions and teaching narratives, or the extended metaphor of priest and victim in the Letter to the Hebrews, without spotting the prominent place accorded to sacrifice in the life and the death of Christ. But to make sacrifice the *central* engine of Christ's atoning work, as does much of classic Reformation doctrine of atonement, threatens to overwhelm and silence the distinctive voice of the Gospel narrative when it tells us with unmistakable force that Jesus was executed on a Roman cross during the Passover festival of the Jews.

Like the cross itself, the Passover is an irreducibly historical and political event, anchored in the statecraft of people and empire of the ancient Near East. The Passover is an irruption of civil strife and rebellion within a dominant empire, Egypt, and the bloody escape of its slaves, a daring flight from slavery, the backbone and hidden cancer of empire. Karl Barth once famously remarked, in his massive Doctrine of Creation in volume three of the *Church Dogmatics*, that the narrative of Holy Scripture does not ignore or undermine Christian attention to the world. Rather, the "world" is included *already* in the domain of Scripture; and the name of the "world" is "Egypt." Nowhere is Barth's insight more fitting, I believe, than in the place of Egypt within the Passover, and in just this way, within the execution of Jesus on the cross. Scripture tells us plainly, it seems to me, that Jesus is a slave, an object and possession, not in a metaphorical or rhetorical fashion only, but rather in full historical seriousness and realism. The Bible is a starkly realistic text and never more so than here. John tells us directly that Jesus is a slave: he stoops down to untie the thong of the disciples' sandals, bathing their feet as does a slave, and teaches them, "A slave is not above his master." The Apostle Paul does not mistake the stern reality of this slavery: his customary opening to his congregations places him with his Master; he is a "slave of Jesus Christ." Just as Jesus drinks the cup of God's fury against the nations, so this Messiah takes on the death of a slave under the reign of the mighty nations of the earth. He, the king, becomes the conscript and forced laborer; he, the Lord of life, becomes the object and lifeless thing that can be tortured to death to remove unpleasantness and inconvenience to

---

6. *Mysterium Paschale: The Mystery of Easter*, trans. Aidan Nichols (Edinburgh: T. & T. Clark, 1990).

the ruling party, a routine matter of discipline in the outposts of empire. As Athanasius said, Jew and Gentile are brought together here, joined in blood and by blood, by a death that can only lay bare, enter into, and testify to the way of nations upon this earth.

Now, such a commentary on Christ's saving work is the stuff of an "exemplarist doctrine of the atonement," a doctrine of Christ's cross that pays special attention to the truth taught, at great cost, by the Truth himself as he goes to his lonely death. Abelard famously expresses such a doctrine in his assertion that our love is awakened by the sight of such terrible suffering by the incarnate Word for the deliverance of sinners. Or, as Schleiermacher would express a similar insight in his systematic work, the *Christian Faith*: our piety is never so stirred and strengthened as when it contemplates Christ in his suffering. Now, a Slave who teaches us in his very torment and death that God will enter into even such corruption to expose it, and take the shame of powerlessness to riddle and overturn the cool pride and contempt of the powerful, is a Teacher who will never be surpassed and whose Voice will never fall silent. And such revelations are of course crucial in any full doctrine of the cross; and theology is not well served, I believe, by an effort to concentrate the mystery of the cross to a single doctrinal focus and account. But a doctrine of the cross of Christ that sees in it *only* an exposure of the cruelty of empires and the venality of the powerful and of the crowd could not hope to rival the richness Holy Scripture offers in the narrative of the Passion, nor the breadth of doctrine Athanasius set out for the church centuries ago. To recover some of this richness for our contemporary theology, we must return to our original question: Why the Roman cross?

Why, we now ask, should the Lord of glory have chosen for himself such a death? Why did the Lord of grace decree and intend the Roman cross of shame? Here I think we may turn with profit to Athanasius' two other reasons for the cross of Christ. You remember that in addition to assigning to the cross a symbolic gesture of reconciling Jew and Gentile in Christ's outspread arms—the reason we have been reflecting upon thus far—Athanasius also assigned to the cross the liberating work of purging the cosmos of evil, as well as taking on, for us and our salvation, the curse, first articulated in Deuteronomy, that falls on those who hang upon the tree. These two reasons are different aspects of the same doctrine of atonement, I believe, and it is this: that in the death of this One Slave, the world's sin became the possession and vestment of the Sinless One; or in more Johannine idiom, in the "hour" of Christ's "lifting up" Satan is cast out and the Son is glorified. At the cross, John testifies, the world has been "overcome." To set out such biblical teaching in contemporary idiom will require us, I believe, to return with even greater intensity to the historical and political realism of slavery and empire. To do so, I should say, entails setting aside one element of our common church tradition—something I do only with reluctance—and one aspect of contemporary theology that has approached near truism in many modern doctrines of atonement: that the death of Christ, and not the particular instrument of that death, is properly the centerpiece of atonement.

If we consider Abelard once again, and the scholastic most often arrayed against him, Anselm of Canterbury, we can see how similar in fact they are to one another—more similar of course than most textbook comparisons allow, which after all are only the wooden framework on which all true theology is built. For both these medievalists, death itself is the *telos*, the goal and purpose, of Christ's work on our behalf; the *manner* of his death, the Roman cross, has no real doctrinal work to do at all. Christ's death, both affirm, had to have been public, visible, costly; unlike Schleiermacher, neither one of these theologians could have imagined a private death as the saving work of our Redeemer. Yet it was no longer in their line of sight to consider the *form* of death as necessary to the redeeming work. Christ could have been stoned or killed by sword, perhaps even by burning. That is because, I believe, the death of Christ, for these theologians, had become a *universal* event, a cosmic one, in which historical particularity was an accidental expression only of the Word who became flesh. We might compare this favorably with the Reformed debates on election or predestination: Just as Christ himself became the means or instrumental cause by which the Father's will for sinners was carried out, so the cross of Christ became the historical means by which the *aim* of atonement, the *death* of Christ, is realized. Any death that awakened the love of ransomed sinners, or completed the perfect and free obedience of the Son of God, would have been the infinitely precious gift that atones for the sin of the world. History itself does not drop away from such a doctrine—that would be a volatilizing of the life of Christ: that heresy modern dogmaticians usually term "gnostic," or in more traditional terms, "docetic." Neither theologian would countenance such an undermining of incarnate history. Yet the death of Christ, just because it is the exclusive and universal aim of the Lord's saving work, renders the cross itself accidental and instrumental; its particular work drops away.

Now, I think a parallel though inverted universalizing can be seen in much modern theology of atonement. For many feminist and liberation theologians, even the death of Christ itself cannot be the aim or purpose of the incarnate Word; rather his *life*, his teaching, his witness, his healing is. But a courageous and faithful person who confronts injustice, who witnesses to the coming reign of God, who denounces suffering and hunger and want: just such a One will die, and usually at the hands of the state. Here the *telos* or aim of Christ's work is his *Person*, his Incarnate *life*, and if the death of Christ becomes the subject of doctrinal elaboration, it is usually assimilated to his Incarnate Person once again. In Kathryn Tanner's words: an incarnational doctrine of the passion shows that death itself is "assumed" by the Word even as humanity in all its misery and need is assumed and healed by the Embodied Son. So, in all these examples, the cross of Christ takes its place in the doctrine of atonement as a means, at times of political will, at times of contingent and accidental history, of enacting the death of the Beloved, the Gift who sets sinners free.

Now it seems to me that Scripture teaches otherwise. I believe the cross itself—the cross *per se*, as a philosopher might say—is vital, essential, and irreducible ingredient in the saving work of Christ. I have tried already to spell out how the cross might *exemplify* the saving work Christ carries out through becoming the slave captured, scorned, tortured, and executed by the Roman Empire. Now I would like to sketch out in a few broad strokes how I believe the cross of Christ might *enact* this saving work, realize it and transact the redemption of the world. In one of Karl Barth's characteristic small asides—those comments that seem at first glance to merely embellish the main point at hand—Barth sets out a distinction that I find both deeply illuminating and powerful. In his famous discussion of nothingness in *Church Dogmatics* III.3, Barth reminds his readers that "being not-God" can have two strikingly different denotations. In one sense, being "not-God" is simply a way of expressing the universal truth that we are creatures, not the Creator; it is what we might call an entirely benign notion of being "not-God," of negativity and finitude. But there is a second denotation, this one far from benign, and this denotation becomes the core to Barth's doctrine of sin and evil. Being "not-God" in this malign sense is being "opposed to God," being a rebel and an enemy of the true Good. In creatures, just this is what we mean by sin, Barth tells us; and in the idiosyncratic and dark form of reality nothingness possesses, not-God is evil itself, that which opposes God and is entirely and victoriously opposed by him. Now I would like to lean upon this distinction Barth has introduced, and put it to our special use here, expanding it with a final form of denotation for the term. In my expanded version I would say that being "not-God" also denotes an entire, complete, and final rejection and annihilation by God: nonbeing in a thorough and absolute and irrevocable sense. This is what I would consider, following the Platonizing tradition in Latin theology, the "privative theory of evil," radicalized and made absolute. I believe a full doctrine of the atonement, then, would illustrate, make use of, and enact this threefold form of "being not-God": of being a creature; of being a rebel against God; and of not-being in any way at all. Holy Scripture tells us, it seems to me, how this threefold nonbeing is borne by and nailed to the cross of Christ.

In the great hymn to the incarnation in the Letter to the Philippians, the Apostle Paul tells us that Christ did not grasp or exploit—the Greek is notorious here—his equality with God, his being in the *morphe theou*, the form of God, but *emptied himself*, taking the form of a slave. From this rich and tantalizing hint of Christology, theologians in the modern era have developed Christologies of haunting power, each exploring in their own key what a self-emptying God might be like and how he might appear among us, his creatures. It seems to me that we might take this verse as well to tell us something concrete and equally haunting about Christ's saving work: he *exchanges*, Paul tells us, the "form of God" for the "form of a slave." Now that exchange—a term already redolent of ancient doctrines of the atonement—Paul characterizes as "emptying," or in my idiom, "being not-God." Now I should be quick to say here that I am not suggesting a doctrine of Christ's Person here! That would be to deny that Christ is fully divine as well as fully human, a position some radical kenoticists might countenance, but they are made of sterner stuff than I. No, I mean rather to apply this term to Christ's saving work, not his Person, a use I believe in fact to adhere more closely to the apostle's own. I believe that we could say that the Eternal Word of God becomes not-God in a benign sense: he becomes a creature, fully human without, as Barth would put this point, ceasing to be God. But in his saving work, he becomes not-God in the malign sense as well; and this is the astonishing good news of Christ's death on Calvary. He becomes sin; he becomes cursed and a curse; he becomes the rebellion against God that is the history of nations and peoples and empires. He becomes a slave. Now, a slave in the ancient world, historians tell us, is something rather different than the slavery we experienced and defended and endured in this nation. Yet even powerful slaves in the ancient world longed for their freedom, and emancipation or redemption was the great lure of army service, as was enslavement by a wealthy owner who could pay the price of freedom. Critical to any experience or definition of slavery, I would argue, is the reality of *being owned*, of being the property of another. Jesus Christ becomes this. He becomes an object, a possession and thing, the living yet lifeless subject of an empire that will sweep its slaves away as so much trash, as offending foreigners who disturb the peace of royal palaces. This is a particular form of nonbeing, and of being not-God: a human status dehumanized, a distillation of the sin and rebellion of nations.

But Jesus becomes not-God in a still more powerful way than this, his *morphe doulous*, the form of a slave. He becomes accursed, hung on the Roman tree. The Apostle Paul, an attentive student of Deuteronomy, recognized this verse as intimating the death Jesus Christ was to die. By the cross, by its public scandal and shame and offense, Jesus becomes the curse that properly belongs to us, his rebel subjects. It is the radicality and dark mystery of this entrance into sin that von Balthasar captures so eloquently and enigmatically in his essay on the atonement, *Mysterium Paschale*. And this mysterious and terrible accursing that becomes Jesus' own is searingly portrayed in Matthew and Mark by the final death agony of this Jewish slave, the "cry of dereliction." On the cross, Christ becomes not-God in this last full measure of sin and defilement; he the Sinless One takes on, assumes, and bears the form of rebellion against God. He tastes death for us all.

But we may reserve our final gratitude for Christ's most radical and gracious act of being not-God, of privation or absolute nonbeing. In Christ's accursed death, I believe we see the depth of this wondrous exchange: Christ annihilates—radically and finally unmakes—the sin of rebels and of nations and empires. Dying as a criminal, the King carries with him into the grave, and enacts the Divine power to completely and absolutely unmake, uncreate, annihilate the forces that rebel against him. As Athanasius said long ago, the Creator is the Redeemer, and this Divine Power, unique to him, is to bring into reality that which is not-God; but it is also unique to him to redeem that creation as well. To redeem that sinful world, the Word and Lord of life becomes the object, the possession and curse that is the very rebellion against him and his reign; and in his death under the form of a slave, he uncreates and annihilates our sin. Through death, he conquers death. This, I believe, is the surpassing wonder of the cross of Christ, the Roman cross of execution.

And so I return to Athanasius, who began our investigation of this holy doctrine. Christ dies on a cross, Athanasius tells us, to bring down the dividing wall between Jew and Gentile; to assume the curse that comes from hanging on the tree; to clear a pathway in the cosmos from sin and demons; and to open the gates of paradise. I have attempted a modern retelling of this great treatise; but by rights the last word belongs to him. Here is Athanasius' final word on the cross of Christ:

> Now if by the sign of the Cross, and by faith in Christ, death is trampled down, it must be evident before the tribunal of truth that it is none other than Christ himself that has displayed trophies and triumphs over death, and made him lose all his strength. . . . For as, if after night-time the sun rises, and the whole region of earth is illumined by him, it is at any rate not open to doubt that it is the sun who has revealed his light everywhere, that has also driven away the dark and given light to all things; so, now that death has come into contempt, and been trodden under foot, from the time when the Savior's saving manifestation in the flesh and his death on the Cross took place, it must be quite plain that it is the very Savior that also appeared in the body, that has brought death to nought, and that displays the signs of victory over him day by day in his own disciples.[7]

---

7. *De Incarnatione*, §29.

4

The Benedictine Jesus

Joseph Bottum

WE'RE IN A PECULIAR situation, right at the moment—or, peculiar, at least, for those who, like all of you, are theologically trained. The most popular, most discussed book about Jesus at the moment is *Jesus of Nazareth*,[1] by Pope Benedict XVI, now in its second part. And what we have with *Jesus of Nazareth* is work I don't know how to describe except as a book of theological Christology.

The trouble is that Benedict insists in the opening pages of this new book of Christology that the one thing he is *not* doing in the book is Christology. No doubt there's a way to square this circle, some theological distinction to be made to save the appearances. But the apparent contradiction raises for us what we might call a question of *audience* for the book, and by answering that question of audience, we may stumble upon resources for understanding both what Pope Benedict's Christology is and why he's now presenting it in what he says is a non-christological form.

I want to try to reach that point with a story, a concatenation, a confabulation of some young people I know, instanced in a young woman named Eleanor, up in New York. As it happens, Eleanor goes to Mass most days. Every day, really, but she feels a little guilty—almost as though it doesn't count—when she misses the early morning service and has to sneak

---

1. *Jesus of Nazareth: Holy Week: From the Entrance into Jerusalem to the Resurrection* (San Francisco: Ignatius, 2011).

away from her coworkers to make the noon Mass at St. Vincent de Paul's on West 23rd.

That's Father Gerald Murray's parish, there in the canyons of Manhattan, its 1930s stone façade pushed out to join the line of the buildings on either side, as flat against the sidewalk as a storefront. No portico, no entryway, no playground, no churchyard: This is a building grimly determined to march out and grab for sacred purposes every inch the freehold and the zoning laws of New York City allow.

St. Vincent's was a French-speaking parish, once upon a time. Back in the days when the French still went to church. Back in the days when the city needed daily Mass for its transient Parisians and United Nations staff. The main Sunday service is still in French—a few dozen Francophone African immigrants in the pews—but the archdiocese has vague plans to close the parish down. They were active plans, in fact, before a new archbishop, a lot more sympathetic to Father Murray's conservatism and pro-life activism, was installed in 2009.

Anyway, Eleanor follows all this stuff: the ins and outs of diocesan politics, the preachers who can be counted upon to deliver orthodox homilies, the priests who can be trusted to perform a Mass with solemnity, significance, and some gesture toward beauty. She'd go to Our Saviour over on Park Avenue for the sermons of Father George Rutler—now *there's* a priest, she thinks, who can be trusted—but it's another fifteen blocks uptown and clear over on the East Side, and she doesn't have time to get there and back in the lunch hour.

So she slips out of the publishing house where she works, copyediting cookbooks and self-help manuals and the kind of small-print puzzle books that turn proofreaders prematurely gray, to walk through the bustle of Chelsea and sit in Father Murray's quiet pews before Mass, reading something—something *serious*, for that's what she is: a mildly pretty twenty-three-year-old, a convert to Catholicism while she was an undergraduate on the Ivy League campus of Dartmouth, and a young woman of deep seriousness.

Almost mad seriousness, in truth. She's not overscrupulous in her morality, or, at least, Christian morality was not the main path for her conversion. It was more of a derived effect of her intellectual alteration, for that's where her seriousness really kicks in: a smart young woman who dresses reasonably well, who goes to the city's concerts and shows, who meets boys and wonders about marriage, who drinks a little and sneaks a cigarette sometimes with her friends, who works long hours in New York City, and who demands that this world—the universe, creation, life, truth, beauty—make sense. Who demands that things cohere. And there she was, the other day, sitting in the pews before Mass, reading Pope Benedict XVI's latest book, *Jesus of Nazareth: Part 2*.

The audience for this book is not you—if you're a theologian or a theologically trained scholar. And yet, at the same time, the audience for *Jesus of Nazareth* is not me, the kind of person who looks for a sweet, somewhat mystical and pre-intellectual work of gentle piety. The audience for what Benedict is now attempting is, instead, someone like Eleanor: a person too young to remember the battles of the 1970s (too smart, for that matter, to remember the battles of the 1970s)—a person who does not understand that scholarship and piety are supposed to be antithetical antipathies, sworn and dedicated enemies, the forms of writing that cannot be joined.

Of course, Benedict had, as Josef Ratzinger, a long history of doing serious theology, and if *Jesus of Nazareth* is not his Christology it is, at least, the fruit of his prior work in the field. The specifically christological aspects of Ratzinger's thought became apparent with his *Introduction to Christianity*, first published in 1969. That book came not long after the Second Vatican Council, a time of two great trends: the tendency in the Church at large to treat everything as up for grabs, and Ratzinger's own reaction against the student upheavals of 1968, which for him clarified all that was at stake in the Church's own upheaval. All of which set the backdrop for what's most distinctive about Ratzinger's Christology: its inseparability from ecclesiology.

Even before the Council had ended, the question arose: if the bishops can change anything in the Church, including her faith, just by getting together and deciding to, why can't the faithful at large? Though counted as one of the progressive experts at the Council, Ratzinger came to reject the premise of the question. He saw that not everything should be, or even could be, up for grabs. Whatever adjustments in pastoral approach seemed necessary, whatever doctrinal developments emerged, the essential identity-in-continuity of the Church and her faith must not only remain, but must be *seen* to remain. And that identity-in-continuity was rooted, ultimately, in the Church's being the Body of Christ, the ordinary sign and instrument of his loving presence in the world.

But that didn't mean the scandal of the Cross would retreat from the Church Militant, the Bride not yet purified for the wedding feast. As Ratzinger wrote in his *Introduction to Christianity*:

Is the Church not simply the continuation of God's deliberate plunge into human wretchedness; is she not simply the continuation of Jesus' habit of sitting at table with sinners, of his mingling with the misery of sin to the point where he actually seems to sink under its weight? Is there not revealed in the unholy holiness of the Church, as opposed to man's expectations of purity, God's true holiness, which is love, love that does not keep its distance in a sort of aristocratic, untouchable purity but mixes with the dirt of the world, in order thus to overcome it? Can, therefore, the holiness of the Church be anything else but the bearing with one another that comes, of course, from the fact that all of us are borne up by Christ?[2]

Ratzinger's ecclesiology, in other words, is no otherworldly triumphalism. The reference he made, in his 2005 homily to the conclave, to the undeniable "filth" in the Church reads almost like an allusion to his language of four decades earlier. For all that, however, he has maintained and even deepened a serene confidence in the identity and value of the troubled, fractious Church. That confidence stems from a theme that was already emerging at the council itself, and would even become the name of a theological journal founded by Ratzinger and his friends soon after the council: *Communio*. That is indeed the unifying theme of Ratzinger's Christology as well as the ecclesiology from which it is inseparable.

Ratzinger crystallized his Christology soon after John Paul II brought him to Rome as head of the Congregation for the Doctrine of the Faith. Thus in 1984, he published a series of meditations called *Behold the Pierced One*.[3] The first and theologically richest part of that work, "Taking Bearings in Christology," is organized around five theses that remain his theses today:

Thesis 1: According to the testimony of Holy Scripture, the center of the life and person of Jesus is his constant communication with the Father.

Thesis 2: Jesus died praying. At the Last Supper he had anticipated his death by giving of himself, thus transforming his death, from within, into an act of love and a glorification of God.

---

2. *Introduction to Christianity*, trans. J. R. Foster (San Francisco: Ignatius, 2004) 342–43.

3. *Behold the Pierced One: An Approach to a Spiritual Christology*, trans. Graham Harrison (San Francisco: Ignatius, 1986).

Thesis 3: Since the center of the person of Jesus is prayer, it is essential to participate in his prayer if we are to know and understand him.

Thesis 4: Sharing in Jesus' praying involves communion with all his brethren. Fellowship with the person of Jesus, which proceeds from participation in his prayer, thus constitutes that all-embracing fellowship that Paul calls "the Body of Christ." So the Church—the Body of Christ—is the true subject of our knowledge of Jesus. In the Church's memory, the past is present because Christ is present and lives in her.

Thesis 5: The core of the dogma defined in the councils of the early Church consists in the statement that Jesus is the true Son of God, of the same essence as the Father and, through the Incarnation, equally of the same essence as us. Ultimately, this definition is nothing other than an interpretation of the life and death of Jesus, which was preordained from the Son's primal conversation with the Father. That is why biblical and dogmatic Christology cannot be divorced from or opposed to one another, no more than Christology and soteriology can be separated. In the same way, Christology "from above" and "from below," the theology of the Incarnation and the theology of the Cross, form an indissoluble unity.

Throughout his career, Ratzinger has consistently said not merely that Jesus remains in intimate relationship with the Father, but that Jesus *is* that relationship between Jesus and the Father. I confess I can't make much sense of that, in a Thomistic way, but clearly it's meant to stress that the fixed identity of Jesus as Son of God is somehow logically equivalent to his dynamic, loving communion with the Father. It's not as though such communion is an optional extra tacked on to the Son's status as Son; the Son exists *by* acting filially toward the Father from all eternity.

That has both soteriological and ecclesiological consequences. Soteriologically, it means that salvation is no mere legal category, such as redemption or imputation, but an ontological reality that makes us participants in the Son's eternal exchange of love with the Father. For that, we must know and love Jesus. And for that knowledge and love, we must belong to his Body, the Church.

Ecclesiologically, therefore, belonging to the Church is not marked by occasional attendance at a clubhouse for the like-minded, still less a mere institutional or cultural affiliation. Celebrating the sacraments, bearing with one another, living the commandments of love, and professing our faith together as members of the Church are nothing less than how we participate in the intimate communion the Son has with the Father. In short, there is for us no Jesus without the Church—the visible Church, with all her flaws, which are as much occasions of grace as her glories.

That approach, developed decades ago, has two epistemological consequences, which the pope emphasizes in the *Jesus of Nazareth* volumes. First, the "Jesus of history" and the "Christ of faith" are identical; second, the "faith" of the Christ of faith is that professed by the Catholic Church, or at least professed in common by those churches that accept all the great "ecumenical" councils of the first millennium. Anything less than that is a serious distortion.

Several centuries of historical-critical exegesis have exposed different strands of tradition, different purposes, and chronological layers of editing in the texts of the canonical Gospels, and questioned the authorship of some letters attributed to Paul. It's hard to say, strictly in terms of exegesis, what "orthodoxy" was for the New Testament church.

Albert Schweitzer pointed out, over a century ago in his *Quest of the Historical Jesus*, that modern exegetes tend to refashion Jesus in their own image; the tendency never quite goes away. Ratzinger noted its return even in the 1950s, on the eve of Vatican II. He is still responding to it, because, thanks to the ever-tempting hermeneutic of suspicion, many no longer trust anything called "the Church" to have preserved the truth about who Jesus was.

Part of the genius of *Jesus of Nazareth* is its idea, and effort to show, that it makes no sense to separate the Jesus of history from the Christ of faith. What makes Jesus different from other rabbis, moral exemplars, and would-be messiahs of his time, and thus a figure of abiding fascination, is how his resurrection from the dead, which the Apostles clearly believed had happened, is connected with the self-consciousness that enabled him to call God *Abba*. The Christology developed in the Church's early centuries is not an effort to gussy up or supplant the experience of Jesus' followers or the facts about him, but precisely to explain them, and hence to explain why we should still care about Jesus more than about anybody else.

Supporting that assertion requires, of course, that showing the Church's memory of Jesus as the Christ of faith is the paradigmatic way for us to know and understand him, and that so much is evident already in the New Testament. Dogma as it has developed over time is not a distortion but an illumination of historical facts. In *Jesus of Nazareth*, Ratzinger illustrates the point, partly by arguing that the Fourth Gospel presupposes, completes, and illuminates the Synoptic Gospels, thus forming rather than detracting from a unitary biblical theology that is coterminous with dogmatic theology.

To generate such an argument with the needed depth and scope, Ratzinger employs "canonical exegesis" rather than limiting himself to the usual historical-critical modes of "source," "form," and "redaction" criticism. From the standpoint of the pure historian or literary critic, of course, that is taking undue liberty with the texts. They call it mere "eisegesis"—an epithet that functions as a shibboleth for the guild. But canonical exegesis makes sense if the Bible is a *canon*, a rule, of faith not just an in-house library.

It makes particular sense for a theologian if, as Ratzinger's CDF argued in 1990, the vocation of the theologian is essentially ecclesial. If the Church is the Body of Christ, then the divine revelation conveyed by her "sources," living Tradition and canonical Scripture, will materially coincide, without being reducible to each other—an implication of Vatican II's dogmatic constitution on divine revelation, *Dei Verbum*, which Ratzinger himself had a hand in drafting.

The point of such an exercise is not primarily apologetic. In keeping with one of his favorite themes, the pope seeks to facilitate in his readers a "personal encounter" with Jesus. Though he denies he is writing a Christology, he spends most of his time on "Christology from below," displaying the "figure" of Jesus. But he does it in such a way as to make it merge with the "message" of Jesus, which is the same as that of the Christ of faith.

And perhaps this is the best way to make sense of someone like Eleanor. (You remember Eleanor, yes? The young woman in those New York pews?) In the public realm of the modern world, the Catholic form of Christianity has come to play a curious role—as though, while Christianity is a faith, Catholicism is an idea. There are a surprising number of these intellectual Catholics out there. A young man named Franciszek, for instance: the Polish boy Eleanor met at a conference on religious liberty and thought it might turn into something, but he went back and entered the seminary in Cracow, after all. Or Peter, who converted at Oxford and who, for John Henry Newman's sake, treks on foot every Sunday from the British Museum to the Brompton Oratory for High Mass.

Or the young classicist Sister John Paul, who gave up her PhD scholarship at the University of Chicago to enter a teaching order in Rome. Or the political theory student Mary Frances, or the aspiring art critic Santiago, or innumerable others: Their faith is real, but that's just the Christianity part. The Catholicism part is the idea, the coherence that comes from two millennia of working out the philosophical and theological implications of that faith, with a large set of social, political, and moral consequences.

And that's what irritates and frightens the hell out of the newspaper editors and the college professors and the political activists—all of religion's cultured despisers, all the people who think they have this modern world wired. *Faith* they can deal with: an illogical remnant of bygone ages, to be admired in other cultures and mocked in our own. But an idea—that's a problem. An idea can change the world.

When the European press deluged the world in 2010 with reporting on priestly crimes, mostly from the 1970s and 1980s, the lesson was not just that members of the Church had done great wrong. Lord knows, they had. But most Catholics understood, as well, that something in the modern world hates the sheer idea of Catholicism—the alternative and the indictment it poses. Indeed, the feeling that Catholics have is one of being under constant attack, as though someone had declared *Ecclesia delenda est.*

The curious thing is that neither the beleaguered Catholic faithful nor the anxious rejecters of religion are wrong, exactly. The public battles over Catholicism during the now fifty years since Vatican II have all been finally a clash of ideas about the modern world—and each side, the Catholic and the anti-Catholic, is death to the other.

John Paul was a philosopher by training, and Benedict is a theologian, and though they differ greatly in the personality of their papacies and the focus of their interests, they share something that Pius XII, John XIII, Paul VI, and even the short-lived John Paul I lacked. The four popes from 1939 to 1978 were all fundamentally churchmen: public intellectuals and commentators, yes, but, at root, they were all trained as bureaucrats for the Church. The two popes since were people who thought first in terms of ideas. They were, in essence, intellectuals, acting on a world stage. They didn't create the Catholic idea, of course, and neither did they bring into existence the intellectual role that Catholicism is playing today in public debates. It was, rather, a case of the times finding the men it required. Or, better, a case of providence: the Holy Spirit guiding the Roman conclave to elect the popes this world most needed.

Of course, the intellectualism is of a somewhat studied kind—a deliberate attempt to reintegrate the divided worlds of faith and modern critical thought. You can see it in the entire life of John Paul, whose greatest work may prove to be his reintegration of the Second Vatican Council into the history of the Catholic Church. Too many Catholics—back in the days when he became pope in 1978—imagined that Vatican II represented a radical break with the past. Some of them wept, and some of them cheered, but whether they were traditionalists on the far right or spirit-of-Vatican-II types on the far left, they all seemed to believe that the new Church was no longer in direct continuity with the old Church.

Part of John Paul's success came simply from the fact that he was able to be a Vatican II Catholic, while drawing deeply on the wells of ancient faith. Remember when the new *Catechism of the Catholic Church* was completed back in 1992? There were those who insisted that Vatican II had produced only such systematic heresy that no catechism was possible, and there were those who insisted that the whole idea of a systematic statement of doctrine and morals had been abolished by the changes in the Church. But John Paul insisted that this new Catechism was possible precisely because the Church remained one in essence with its past—indeed, that the Catechism was indispensable "in order that all the richness of the teaching of the Church following the Second Vatican Council could be preserved in a new synthesis and be given a new direction."[4]

A precise parallel is what Benedict XVI is trying to achieve with his new book. The news reports have concentrated on the flashy but mostly incidental moments in the text—where the pope rejects the idea that Jesus was a revolutionary aiming at the political overthrow of Jerusalem's Roman overlords, for instance. Or the passage in which he seems to gesture toward Islamist terrorism: "The cruel consequences of religiously motivated violence are only too evident to us all," he notes. "Violence does not build up the kingdom of God, the kingdom of humanity. On the contrary, it is a favorite instrument of the Antichrist, however idealistic its religious motivation may be." Indeed, "It serves, not humanity, but inhumanity."[5]

Some attention has been paid to the passage where Benedict discusses the need for Christians to "visibly" unite—an Associated Press writer calling it "a veiled call for other Christians to convert to Catholicism." And then there's all the notice given to the parts of the book where Benedict affirms the teaching of Vatican II's *Nostra Aetate* in rejecting the notion that the Jews were responsible for the death of Jesus. Indeed, in the first instance,

---

4. *Crossing the Threshold of Hope*, ed. Vittorio Messori, trans. Jenny McPhee and Martha McPhee (New York: Knopf, 1994) 164. Italics in original.

5. *Jesus of Nazareth*, 15.

"the circle of accusers who instigate Jesus' death is precisely indicated in the Fourth Gospel and clearly limited: it is the Temple aristocracy."

All of this is interesting, of course, but the real effect of this second part of *Jesus of Nazareth* lies in the technique the pope employs. The pious readers seem to have a little trouble with the scholarly tone of the book, and the scholarly readers have loudly proclaimed their distaste for the pious tone of the book.

In *The Guardian*, for instance, Geza Vermes, professor emeritus of Jewish studies at Oxford, sniffs, "The pope's treatment of 'the figure and the words of the Lord' consists of mountains of pious and largely familiar musings. He provides unquestioning Christians with plenty of solace." And as for Benedict's scholarship, well, "Gospel experts . . . may note with pleasure that 200 years of labour has not been in vain and that small fragments of New Testament criticism seem to have penetrated the mighty stronghold of traditional Christianity."[6]

All that comes to, in the end, is proof that such readers are still mired in the 1970s. It's the pope who has successfully managed to move on. It's Benedict XVI who has succeeded in marrying what the 1970s thought impossible: biblical faith and biblical scholarship. He has mastered and now presents to the world the technique of reading *with* the tradition of the Church. It's the historical-critical method, without the pseudoscientific suspicion that was once thought the vital core of the discipline. In fact, that kind of suspicion proved a dead end for much theological work—a false light that led nowhere.

Benedict will win no prizes for his prose, but he has the better lantern, and he's leading the reader toward a place where the work of scholarship and the truth of faith are not defined as opposed. Watch, for instance, how he turns the discussion of the Jews that has received so many news reports. "When in Matthew's account the 'whole people' say: 'His blood be on us and on our children' (27:25), the Christian will remember that Jesus' blood speaks a different language from the blood of Abel (Heb 12:24): it does not cry out for vengeance and punishment; it brings reconciliation. It is not poured out *against* anyone; it is poured out *for* many, for all."[7]

When we read in the light of faith, what Matthew means is that "we all stand in the need of the purifying power of love which is his blood. These

---

6. Review of *Jesus of Nazareth: Holy Week*, *The Guardian*, March 11, 2011. Online: http://www.guardian.co.uk/books/2011/mar/12/jesus-nazareth-pope-benedict-review.

7. *Jesus of Nazareth*, 187.

words are not a curse, but rather redemption, salvation. Only when understood in terms of the theology of the Last Supper and the Cross, drawn from the whole of the New Testament, does this verse from Matthew's Gospel take on its correct meaning."[8]

John Paul II was always two steps ahead of his critics, escaping the locked-down, either-or categories into which they tried to push him by finding the new, both-and possibilities that come from integrating Vatican II into the long tradition of the Church. Which is precisely what, in his writing, Benedict XVI is up to. *Jesus of Nazareth* is a promise that the intellectual life is not divorced from the life of faith and the scholarly pursuit is not the enemy of piety. It's an idea, in the end—a claim that God exists, that Christ is real, and thus that the world makes a kind of unified sense. That, as young Eleanor so devoutly wishes, things really do cohere.

One sometimes wishes the Vatican itself would get the news of what this pope is doing. From the ginned-up Muslim reaction to a scholarly passage in Benedict's 2006 Regensburg lecture to the 2010 reporting on the priest scandals, the Vatican bureaucracy has lurched from one mismanaged crisis to another. Perhaps there was some benefit to the old style of pope, who understood how to rule. Neither the last pope nor this one qualifies as an even vaguely competent manager of the bureaucratic side of the job.

Of course, John Paul II had an alternative: Jetting back and forth around the world, his personal magnetism served as a kind of quasi-Vatican. Simply by the sheer star-power of his personality, he carried Catholicism forward. Benedict has proved quite charming in his public appearances, but it is a quieter sort of charm, more a twinkle than a blaze. And when combined with his age, his much more retiring nature, and his scholarly interest, he lacks the resources that John Paul II had for putting his vision before the public eye.

That's what makes a book like *Jesus of Nazareth* so important: *This* is where Benedict is doing his work. The book is the equivalent of John Paul II's personal appearances, teaching the new vision of a Church in which the best of the modern joins without contradiction the best of the past—all in order to offer the world an *idea*. A coherent alternative.

From the perspective of Eleanor, sitting in the pews of New York's St. Vincent de Paul parish, waiting for the noon Mass to begin, it's all the better that the result is exactly what she loves: a book. A pious thing to read. A smart thing to read.

8. Ibid., 187–88.

5

"Lord, to Whom Shall We Go? You Have the Words of Eternal Life"

Jesus as Lord in Prayer and Pastoral Care

Kathryn Greene-McCreight

> Almighty and everliving God, ruler of all things in heaven and on earth, hear our prayers for [our] parish [families]. Strengthen the faithful, arouse the careless, and restore the penitent. Grant us all things necessary for our common life, and bring us all to be of one heart and mind within your holy Church; through Jesus Christ our Lord. *Amen.*[1]

I FIND MYSELF FACED with the impossible task of speaking on a topic I did not choose, which I tried to trade for another, and about which I know relatively little. That is: "Jesus as Lord in prayer and pastoral care". What I do know about prayer is mostly what I have learned by dint of sheer necessity during several illnesses throughout my adult life in which, quite literally, the only way I could hang on was by praying. Especially this year, my prayers have often been entirely ungrateful bursts of screaming, spitting, cussing. And that has been when I have even been able to pray. The only thing that has redeemed this God-awful prayer is the fact that I have had precious few

---

1. *Book of Common Prayer*, "Prayers for the Church," #11, "For the Parish," 817.

words of my own to pray. The words that have filled my prayers have been from the psalmist, the whole canon of Scripture, the Book of Common Prayer, and the Great Cloud of Witnesses upon whose shoulders we are privileged to sit. So I shall not pretend to speak to you as an expert on the experience of prayer.

But to say that I know nothing of prayer is not entirely true. My father, now of blessed memory, will always remain for me a model of a shepherd of his flock and, in a way, of prayer. Even so, he was not exactly what I would call a man of prayer in his outward life. Dinner blessings were always rote, quickly delivered, and always presided over by him. He did not encourage his family to make daily prayers and supplications for the needs of the world. He was never the one to tuck us in at night and say our prayers with us. This was always my mother's responsibility. And, because he was a Congregational pastor, my father did not have recourse to the Book of Common Prayer as guide.

From my earliest memories, however, his Sunday worship pastoral prayers were never written out. They were always off the cuff. But they were never trite, never shallow. They were always profound, reflecting that "deep calling to deep." You could tell from his body and his face as he prayed, if you dared so much as to open your eyes during the pastoral prayer, that he was wrestling with the Holy One of Israel. Here he was, another Jacob at the Jabbok. My dad's face and body would testify to the struggle. After he died, one of his colleagues remarked on this: "While most pastors bow their head piously when they pray, often reading a prayer, your father would throw back his head, and turn his face to the heavens, as if searching for Jesus himself seated at the right hand of the Father."

I should add at this point that, while I am convinced that my father was in the hands of the Lord in this spontaneous prayer, I myself am often suspicious of off-the-cuff prayers. Especially when they do not rely on Scripture, but rest more on the feelings of the pastor or priest. Or worse still, resting on how she is trying to get the congregation to feel. This probably says more about my own distrust of feelings in general. I find feelings to be dangerous, if not also sometimes tools of the Tempter. Also, I have been the unhappy witness to more than one or two pastoral prayers offered by clergy during worship in which it was apparent that the pastor was *not* praying to God. On such occasions the minister was either lecturing the congregation, or worse, lecturing the Almighty *ad infinitum*. Without a guide, one tends not to know when to finish. If you are going to fake praying in public, at least make it short.

As I see it, prayer itself is not an "experience" in the day-to-day use of the term. Maybe even more importantly, prayer is not a "life." I have been asked from time to time about my prayer "life," and have always been rather puzzled to hear that there is a "life" to prayer distinct from every other moment of one's life. Prayer is a discipline. It is in an act of obedience to our Lord's command that we "pray always and never lose heart" (Luke 18:1).

I remember a seminarian who had recently become rector of a small but active parish. She confessed to me her horrible "prayer life." I asked her to say more. Evidently she felt that she never could find the time for the Daily Office in her busy day. I asked if she could simply instruct her secretary to hold all calls and visitors for the first hour that she was in the office. That way, she could at the very least carry out the discipline of Morning Prayer. She looked at me as though I were from Mars. I clearly did not understand her dilemma. She was a Very Busy Rector. I told her that we all make our choices, and that her choice was clearly not to have a disciplined "prayer life." And yet what does our Lord tell the disciples while he himself was praying in Gethsemane the night before he went to the Cross? "Stay here, and keep watch with me. . . . Stay awake and pray that you may not come into the time of trial" (Matt 26:38, 41).

Prayer may begin with thoughts (and probably will). And it may provoke thoughts in us. Prayer will clearly use our cognition. But primarily prayer is not about thoughts either. Prayer is a willed address to God the Father through the Son in the power of the Holy Spirit. And it is through this discipline that we come to know and therefore to love the triune God.

But of course prayer is not only an address, a yakking away at God. It is also sitting and waiting on the Holy One. This is true of course for the individual lay Christian, but even more so for the pastor or priest. I think of Samuel as he played intermediary between the people and the LORD in 1 Samuel 8. Israel wanted to be "like the other nations," and they pleaded with Samuel for a king. Samuel first listened to the people, then reported their words "in the ears of the LORD," waited for the LORD's response, and gave the response to the people. This back-and-forth bore fruit in the anointing of King David. If Samuel had just told the LORD what the people wanted, and not waited on the LORD's reply, there would have been no King David. We should remember this when we are tempted to understand intercession as simply ticking off the names of the sick and the suffering in our parish.

Who Do You Say That I Am?

I am reminded of John Cage's famous composition in three movements: 4 minutes and 33 seconds of "silence." His point (if a composer can be said to have a point) is that there is never just silence. Always somewhere there is sound. So, we might in like manner say of God that God is never silent, and listening to the voice of God may occasionally require little more than turning down the noise in our souls. *Stay here and wait with me.*

So, while I admit that I know little about prayer, I would add the *caveat* that as I see it, pastoral care and prayer cannot be separated—neither one from the other, nor from the Lordship of Jesus. How can the pastor or priest care for a flock without praying for the flock as a whole, or for the individual sheep? What is pastoral care that does not include guiding each sheep, and the flock as a whole, into the discipline of prayer? Furthermore, I would ask: what is pastoral care without the shepherd's own discipline of prayer? Consider the Lord Jesus, how he himself prayed, and taught his disciples to pray: "Our Father, who art in heaven . . ."

As I thought about how I might structure my remarks here, I thought about arranging my reflections on prayer and pastoral care around Jesus' work: His incarnation, cross, resurrection, ascension, session at the right hand of the Father, and his coming in glory to judge the quick and the dead. However, I found my thoughts focusing mostly around the cross. And this may say more about me than about Christian pastoral care and prayer *per se*.

I am not intending to suggest that Jesus' incarnation, resurrection, ascension, and judgment are not also crucial for the formation of our pastoral care and prayer. But these are his and, for the most part, his alone. Yes, the cross too is his. But it is also ours, especially during our earthly lives. "Whoever does not take up his cross and follow me is not worthy of me" (Matt 10:38; 16:24, par.). Here the possessive pronoun "his" (*autou*) stands after the noun for cross (*ton stauron*) in the Greek text, as one would expect. The RSV translates the pronoun "his" also as one would expect. But the NRSV leaves out the possessive pronoun, and substitutes for it the definite article. So, "*his* cross" becomes "*the* cross."

I imagine this was done with the best of intentions, in order to avoid the charge of sexism with the use of the masculine possessive pronoun. But we lose the force of Jesus' statement if we leave out the possessive pronoun, even if only in order not to offend. The cross we are to pick up is not just Jesus' cross. Neither is it simply a generic cross, as though the cross were one of the universal structures of human consciousness, or even of human existence. Our cross is *ours*, but it is only ours in his. Ours is the cross belonging to the follower of the Crucified Jesus.

And what did Jesus tell us the night before he went to his own cross? That it would define how he loves, and thus how we are to love one another. "I give you a new commandment, that you love one another as I have loved you" (John 13:34). That commandment of course is not entirely new, for we find it in Leviticus, where Jesus himself would certainly have found it. The positive command follows a negative command and ends with the grounding reality of both: "You shall not take vengeance or bear a grudge against any of your people, but you shall love your neighbor as yourself: I am the LORD" (Lev 19:18). This venerable old command, though, is given a specific pointedness in Jesus' self-giving on the cross. Jesus commands us to love one another as he has loved us. Realistically, now, how are we to do that? Surely he can't be serious? This new command should shake us to the very soles of our feet.

And so, again I think of my father of blessed memory. He knew not only how to pray for his flock, but also how to give of himself in love for his sheep. The oldest member of the flock entrusted to my father was ninety-three years old at the time of the great ice storm of 1976. Snowstorms, even the deepest, are preferable to ice storms. During the storm, the furnace in this woman's home broke down. For some reason (which was clearly not important to me, because I do not remember it), the repair service would not come out to her home right away. My father tried repeatedly to convince her to stay at our home until they could send a repair service. She would not budge. "I am ninety-three years old. If I leave my home, I will never return." But this is important, and therefore I do remember it: my father drove his little red VW bug, slithering up that steep hill to her home. He did this every five hours throughout that day and night to put another log on her fire so she would not freeze to death. She survived that ice storm under a pile of blankets in her comfy chair right next to her fireplace. That is the model of pastoral care I had as a child. Such self-giving care is never delivered on our own steam, but is a gift we shepherds receive at the foot of the cross of the Lamb of God.

When my father retired, his successor for some reason wanted to meet with me. He asked me what I thought my father's greatest strength was as pastor of that congregation. I told him that my father really loved the people. "All pastors love their flock," he replied. "But no," I insisted, "my father really *loved* his flock." Dad's successor just stared at me, dumbfounded.

Who Do You Say That I Am?

Taking up our cross and following Jesus means that we Christians, lay or ordained, must give ourselves over to our Lord with a single-minded devotion completely unlike that demanded in any other profession. Jesus says, "Whoever loves father or mother more than me is not worthy of me" (Matt 10:37). Ouch. Such fanaticism, the world would say! And maybe we, too, would want to join in that assessment.

As we consider what it means to take up our cross, I would have us look to four interchanges between our Lord and his friends. Each of these interchanges centers in some way on Jesus' cross. Each sketches for us Jesus' identity. They are found in Matthew 16, John 6, Matthew 11 (cf. Luke 7), and John 11.

The first is a question Jesus asks: "But who do you say that I am?" (Matt 16:15). This is, of course, the question that supplies the title of our conference. Jesus does not direct this question at Peter alone. It might seem that way in the English translations. But the word behind the *you* is not the second person singular pronoun. In Greek, it is the plural form of the second person pronoun, *humeis*. In English this pronoun can be translated with the second person pronoun as either singular or plural (except perhaps in the South: *y'all*). But in many other languages, especially European languages, this difference is apparent: *Tu/vous, tu/ustedes* (or *vosotros*, depending on the country), *du/Sie* . . . So, Jesus directs his question, "Who do you say that I am?" to the disciples as a body. It is Peter who answers for the group: "You are the Messiah, the Son of the Living God" (v. 16). As we read this interchange in Matthew, we are given our own answer. Just as catechisms follow their question and answer format, so Jesus' question and Peter's response form for us our own little catechesis. And so we as Christians don't get to make up our answer to this question. Jesus' identity is so overpowering and elicits a response that is so self-involving, that Peter's response to Jesus' question is a template for us. Because we read this interchange in Scripture, we know that Jesus' question is directed not only to the disciples gathered there in the first century at Caesarea Philippi, but to us even in the twenty-first century.

The second interchange is in many ways similar. Jesus' question about his own identity directed to the disciples in Matthew 16 comes to us again in a different guise in John 6. There Jesus says that his own flesh is similar to, and yet distinct from, the manna given to our ancestors in the desert. "I am the living bread that came down from heaven. Whoever eats of this bread will live for ever; and the bread that I will give for the life of the world is my flesh" (v. 51). This statement is followed soon after by the response of many of the disciples: "This teaching is difficult; who can accept it?" (v. 60). Jesus then asks, "Does this offend you?" (v. 61). The text notes that "many of his disciples turned back and no longer went about with him" (v. 66). Jesus addresses the Twelve, asking, "Do you also wish to go away?" (v. 67). This too we need to hear as directed to us. Again, Peter answers for the Twelve: "To whom can we go? You have the words of eternal life" (v. 68).

And as we grapple with what prayer and pastoral care would mean if Jesus' cross is our fulcrum, we must ask ourselves and one another: does this difficult teaching (or maybe better: prophecy) about Jesus giving his flesh for the life of the world offend *us*? Do *we* also want to go away? To whom else, where else, could we ever go? If we leave him, we are, so to speak, cutting off our nose to spite our face. *He* has the words of everlasting life.

The third interchange, like the first, is a question, but this one is on the lips of John the Baptist's disciples (Matt 11:2–6 and Luke 7:18–23). Some of them want to know the exact nature of Jesus' identity: "Are you the One who is to come, or are we to wait for another?" Jesus answers, drawing on the words of the prophet Isaiah (see Isa 29:18; 42:7; 61:1): "The blind receive their sight, the lame walk, the lepers are cleansed, the deaf hear, the dead are raised, and the poor have good news preached to them." And then Jesus gives the conclusion: "Blessed is the one who takes no offense at me." I often think of Jesus' statement here when we complain about the offensiveness of Jesus—his maleness, his Jewishness, his life in an ancient time and a faraway land . . . But blessed are we when we take no offense at him.

Before considering the fourth interchange framing Jesus' identity, we should take a short detour here. We ought to ask ourselves, how are we to set ourselves up for the greatest possible degree of success in avoiding our own taking offense at Jesus? I would send us back to prayer. Paul sets out for himself as preacher in 1 Corinthians 9:24–27 the image of the athlete in training. Granted, he is speaking here specifically of preaching, but since, as I have said, I don't put much stock in segregating neatly the pastoral duties one from another, the analogy is useful also as regards the duty of prayer. "Do you not know that in a race the runners all compete, but only one receives the prize? Run in such a way that you may win it. Athletes exercise self-control in all things; they do it to receive a perishable wreath, but we an imperishable one. So I do not run aimlessly, nor do I box as though beating the air; but I punish my body and enslave it, so that after proclaiming to others I myself should not be disqualified." The exercise of prayer is what can keep our eyes fixed on Jesus, and will prevent us from taking offense at him.

Later in that same letter, Paul says, "No testing has overtaken you that is not common to all. God is faithful, and he will not let you be tested beyond your strength, but with your testing will also provide the way out so that you may be able to endure it" (1 Cor 10:12–13). There are times when I have seriously questioned Paul's sanity here. How can it be that we are not tested beyond our strength? I myself have been perilously close to that "beyond." The only thing that has kept me from tumbling out into that "beyond" is following a strict discipline of prayer, as athletes follow their training schedules. And the converse is true as well. When I am not disciplined in prayer, I stumble. I take offense. But acknowledging Jesus as Lord, fixing our gaze on his body on that cross, allows us to be *us*. He relieves us of the burden of trying to be him.

We are reminded that Jesus relieves us of the burden of being anything else other than ourselves in the Letter to the Hebrews. Jesus, it tells us, went behind the curtain to the Mercy Seat once *for all* (Heb 9:12). *Once* for all. This means that we don't have to go there. Our taking up our own cross is how we participate in his suffering. But our participation is (of course) not salvific. His cross saves the world. Ours does not even save us. We are not little Jesuses. Mercifully. We must check our Messiah complexes at the door.

Yes, it is true that the good pastor will need to be comfortable with being needed. The good pastor will neither despise nor flee from the exigencies of pastoral work. But the good pastor must always point, as did John the Baptist, to Jesus: "He must increase, but I must decrease" (John 3:30). This is one of the most important defining statements about the Christian life for us all, lay or ordained. And I find it to be one of the most "difficult teachings."

I dabbled during my undergraduate years in the study of languages. One of these, in which I made little progress, was ASL: American Sign Language. I don't remember much of it, but I do remember the sign for *Jesus*. It is this: we point with each middle finger in turn to the opposite palm of each hand, as though tracing on our palms his wounds. The sign for *Christian* is related to this: first we make the sign for Jesus, then the sign for *person*, which is both hands at our sides, moving downward. Wounds-person. Cross-person.

Notice how the cross becomes more of a verb than a noun. We mark Jesus' wounds, as though engraving them on the palms of our hands. As a sign that God has not abandoned Israel even in their exile, just as a nursing mother cannot forget her infant, so God promises that he holds them inscribed in the palm of his hand (Isa 49:16). God in the cross engraves us in the palm of his hand by the saving wounds of Christ. *His* flesh and *his* wounds define ours. Pastoral care thus means assuring our flock that we are as a body engraved on the palms of God's hands. And thus our flock should be engraved on our palms as well.

And so we remember a fourth interchange, this one between Jesus and Mary and Martha at the so-called raising of their brother Lazarus in John 11. We know that the verse markings were added to the biblical text as late as the twelfth century. Yet it was clearly the wisdom of that Great Cloud of Witnesses who went before us that we read of Jesus' act in John 11:35 in the terse, pointed sentence, "Jesus wept." Bible trivia games ask us, "What is the shortest verse in the Bible?" Here it is: John 11:35, "Jesus wept." He displays compassion, but even more: unadulterated grief at the loss of his dear friend Lazarus. And this episode of Jesus' very human emotion comes to us in the Gospel according to John, which is usually known for its emphasis on Jesus' divinity.

Both Mary and Martha, at different points in the story, complain to him, "Lord, if you had been here, my brother would not have died" (vv. 21 and 32). These statements are not really a complaint, a "Where were you when we needed you?" More to the point, these words confirm Mary's and Martha's faith. And thus ours too. Jesus himself announces, "I am the resurrection and the life" (v. 25). He is the one who could have prevented Lazarus' death. Both of the sisters realize this. But he didn't do this for a reason, for our benefit. He postpones his arrival at the home of Lazarus so that raising his friend would serve as a *sign*, a pointer to his identity. But even the knowledge that his delay was necessary for them and for us does not erase his grief.

The term *sign* appears throughout the Gospel according to John, while the word *miracle* tends to function in a similar way in the Synoptics. Both words point to Jesus' identity more than they do to his actions. Jesus is not merely another miracle worker from the ancient Near East. These seem to have been a dime a dozen. The *sign* of John 11 reveals him to be who he is, the resurrection and the life.

Notice, by the way, that Jesus doesn't exactly *raise* Lazarus in John 11. Rather, he gives a simple command: "Lazarus, come forth!" And the text then says: "The dead man came out" (v. 44). The *sign* Jesus makes is not that he gives Lazarus a resurrection to new life. Lazarus will die again; Jesus' act here is more of a resuscitation than it is a raising to new life. Resurrection will be the case for Jesus himself, but of course only after his cross. And he promises this eternal life to us as well, but only insofar as we are in him, as we participate in his cross.

The sign in John 11 points to Jesus' very identity: he is the one who makes the dead, not the living, come out of tombs. Now, *there* is a stunt. Our flocks are composed of dead bodies that Jesus is calling forth from the tombs. And we too are named among those dead bodies. How can we not have compassion on those whose tombs we share? If we are to follow our Lord, who entered into the grief of those whom he called his friends, we must see our own pastoral care as a participation in not only the joys and delights of our flock, but also in their griefs and sorrows.

But (a big *but*!) pastoral care can never involve making it "all better." We can't do that, nor should we ever pretend that we could. Our flock may expect us to be able to make it all better. But that is Jesus' job. Again, we must point away from ourselves to him. The only way to begin to speak to human pain, even just to speak one word to those who suffer, is to point to that Man of Sorrows on the cross. It is the only way I know how.

In her book *The Year of Magical Thinking*,[2] Joan Didion describes her own grief following the death of her husband. She illustrates how human suffering can often be experienced as sporadic. She points out how her grief and feelings of loss came in spurts, in short moments of excruciating loneliness and desire for her dead husband. While often she was able to lose herself in the ordinary and everyday, from time to time her grief would burst forth into her awareness—and would burn like fire.

And so also with us, pain is sporadic. Thank God. If it were not sporadic, we would surely not survive it. This you can remind your flock when they go through pain. The pain is real. The pain is deep. It hurts. But it *will* go away. It may come again, but pain's searing quality will dissipate at least a bit over time. I am *not* suggesting that we give that old platitude: "Time heals all wounds." I am not sure that time really heals all wounds anyway. After all, the scars of Jesus' crucifixion remain on his resurrected body. Hence the ASL sign for *Jesus*. But they don't seem to hurt him anymore. He

---

[2] *The Year of Magical Thinking* (New York: Knopf, 2006).

shows no apparent pain when Thomas probes them for proof. Nevertheless, they remain visible and tangible. That should be a lesson to us in our pastoral care. The scars from the pain of our fallen world will remain in our hearts and bodies, and yet even that pain is sanctified in him.

I remember caring for my mother as she lay dying, in her final days battling cancer. One afternoon just days before the end, somehow her pain had became unmanageable. As I gave her an extra dose of morphine, her eyes searched my face in panic. "When will the pain go away?" she rasped. Now, clearly, I am not a nurse. I am a doctor of Christian theology, not medicine. (As my son once quipped: "You are the kind of doctor who doesn't do anybody any good, Mom.") But I knew I had to answer my own mother's question, and I knew I had to be quick. So I made it up: "Six minutes."

I would *not* recommend saying what you don't really know in order to address the concerns of pastoral care. But we must gently remind our sheep who suffer that pain is sporadic. With my mom, I was right. Within five minutes, she nodded her head, eyes closed, and told me in a relieved tone that the morphine was beginning to take effect. Those were the last words I would hear my mother say.

But: six minutes? How was I right? I had experience from giving her the morphine over the previous days of her increasing suffering. I knew by then roughly how long it took to work. So I did not exactly make it up. My point here is that for effective and faithful pastoral care, we must have experience with those under our care. We must bear with them their cross. We must be to them a Simon of Cyrene, who at cost to himself helped bear even our Lord's cross.

But of course, the cross is not only pain and suffering. It is this only to those who do not grasp its scope and profundity. To say that we would not know the resurrection without the cross is close to this, but only in a shallow and plastic sense. Pain is not the opposite of joy, but reveals joy to be what it is. It is this twin aspect to true charity that makes love both beautiful and haunting at the same time. Excruciating pain and deepest love are borne together. Any new mother of an infant will attest to this. While the world may see the cross as pain alone, cross-persons must not. And we need to remind our flock of this. The joy of the cross does not await our own earthly demise. The joy of the cross is not found only after the resurrection. We find it even in our "now," even in shadows cast behind us by the light of our risen Lord. *Unless you take up your cross and follow me, you are not worthy to be my disciples.* And such joy there is in being counted worthy, especially in being counted worthy to suffer on account of the gospel, says Paul.

I remember the words of a hymn from my childhood, "In the Cross of Christ I Glory." I leave you here with verse 4:

> Bane and blessing, pain and pleasure,
> By the cross are sanctified;
> Peace is there that knows no measure,
> Joys that through all time abide.[3]

Take up your cross, and follow.

---

3. John Bowring (1792–1872).

6

Proclaiming the Lord Jesus Christ

Fleming Rutledge

THE TITLE THAT WAS suggested to me was simply "Proclaiming Jesus." I have amended it to "Proclaiming [or Preaching] *the Lord Jesus Christ*," for reasons which I trust will become clear as we proceed. I propose to divide my time as follows: first, a presentation, and then an actual sermon.

I've been set here in a constellation of stellar theologians, where I do not really belong, but for which I'm very grateful. I'm not an academic theologian; I'm here as a preacher. I think I should explain that this presentation is a commentary from a Protestant perspective. It would be presumptuous for me to comment on Roman Catholic preaching, because I haven't had enough experience with it. However, if you add up the numbers of *Protestant* sermons I've heard in my seventy-four years of faithful churchgoing all over this country in all the major denominations, it would be a fair sample of what's going on in the pulpits.

At the same time, I'm not a member of the American Academy of Homiletics, and I haven't much interest in theories about preaching. The best writers know that theories don't help much when it comes to putting across a story. It's interesting that *The Good Earth*, by Pearl Buck, has made a modest comeback after fifty years of near-total eclipse and much critical disdain for being, among other literary sins, "plot driven." It seems that plots might not be such a hopelessly retrograde idea after all. In my files I have an article about a much-admired Argentinean writer, Marcelo

Birmajer, who is known for his straightforward narrative writing, very different from that of older Latin American writers like García Márquez and Vargas Llosa. He says this: "What I like the most is to sit around the fire, so to speak, and tell a story. . . . The story of Solomon, of David, of Pesach, the Torah itself, all are stories with a beginning, middle and end. So all this stuff of postmodernism and literary experimentation and vanguards aren't worth a shekel to me. I never experiment with structure."[1]

He never experiments with structure! We can take that to mean that preachers and biblical interpreters should have more respect for the biblical narrative and stop worrying about the latest hermeneutical or homiletical notions. Here's a truly radical notion: even if we are burned-out preachers and can't, or don't, *believe* what the Bible is saying, we can still listen to the text on its own terms. We do this as though we were an adult reading a fairy story to a child. If we hear, or tell, the story in that way, the Bible begins to speak in the way it means to be heard. Paul Ricoeur refers to reading in this sort of way as "the second naïveté." He writes, "Beyond the desert of criticism, we wish to be called again."[2] Worn-out or jaded preachers who follow this path of trusting what they do not really believe might find themselves converted, or reconverted, by their own preaching. Stranger things have happened! After all, if we believe what the church has always said about the Word of God, it will not be so surprising if it turns out to create faith where there was no faith—even in the preacher himself. This is the foundation of preaching: the unique capacity of the Word of God working through the biblical story.

But what story, exactly, does the Bible tell? There's the rub. Most of us in the church have been so deeply affected by cultural trends that we don't realize how far we've drifted from the central message. The Bible is not a story of a search for God, or a history of the religious consciousness of the Hebrew people, or a guide to human spiritual development. It is not an all-purpose resource for our needs in the usual sense. Everyone in the churches these days seems to be talking about his or her spiritual journey—but the fundamental story of the Bible is not about *our* journey at all. It's about what Barth calls "the journey of the Son of God into the far country." That's the story we're called to preach, but it's extremely difficult in today's

---

1. Larry Rohter, "An Argentine with Literary Roots in Singer and Roth," *New York Times*, January 29, 2005. Online: http://www.nytimes.com/2005/01/29/movies/29embr.html?_r=0.

2. *The Symbolism of Evil* (Boston: Beacon, 1969), 349.

environment for us to keep our eyes on that story. With very few exceptions, the voices we hear are asking us to recast the biblical story in *anthropological* terms instead of *theo*logical terms, so that we do this habitually without even thinking about it. It takes a lot of training, determination, and perseverance for a preacher to overcome these ubiquitous urgings.

I've preached from the lectionary almost all my preaching life, but in recent years, I've begun to wonder if the old practice of preaching through an entire book wasn't better. Every Sunday in many churches, we see the Old Testament and Epistle passages read from little pieces of paper and the Gospel read from a so-called Gospel book—which is actually not Gospel at all but selections from those books. We might ask ourselves if we haven't unwittingly produced congregations of people who can't handle the actual Bible, and a generation of preachers who preach exclusively from preselected excerpts. Some years ago a preacher from one of the conservative denominations said to a group of clergy that he wouldn't dream of beginning a sermon on a given text until he had reread the entire biblical book that it came from. At the time I thought he was exaggerating, but now I see the wisdom in what he said. Of course we know that the Synoptic Gospels were originally made up of pericopes, small units of text suitable for declaiming in worship, but the evangelists—whoever they were—have shaped the oral tradition in specific ways to tell us something necessary about Jesus of Nazareth, and we can only understand this if we read the whole product of each Evangelist.

In preparation for this presentation, therefore, I decided to take my own advice and read a whole book at one long sitting. In recent years I've preached almost exclusively from the Old Testament and Paul's Epistles (partly as a protest against the practice in my denomination of preaching almost exclusively from the Gospels), so this time I chose the Gospel of Matthew. I tried to read Matthew through two lenses simultaneously, *both* the "historical" lens *and* the lens of the "second naïveté." Only if one has been thoroughly trained in the historical-critical method can one speak of the second naïveté. We can't cultivate a false innocence, as though we were untouched by the scientific method. When one has passed through that stage and has sensed its inadequacy for preaching and understanding, one may then receive the text in a fresh way.

Here's what I received. The Gospel of Matthew lives, breathes, and pours out its summons. Its entire purpose is that we should see and believe that Jesus of Nazareth is Messiah and Son of God (in the words of Peter's confession, "You are the Christ, the Son of the living God"). Taking bits and pieces of the Sermon on the Mount, or the parables, in isolation from Matthew's central message does violence to the intention of the evangelist. It's so important for us to understand that. One does not have to *believe* Matthew's claim in order *to understand what it is*. One may find the stories strange, or perplexing, or unconvincing. One may point out the inconsistencies and conclude that no one living in today's world can believe such stories. These are genuine responses. But what one may *not* do, it seems to me, is make out the four Gospels to be something that they manifestly are not. Approaching a text for preaching, we may think it does not "turn to the listener" in the way we would like, so we try to figure out a way to make it palatable, or relevant, or accessible. The problem is that if we overdo that, it violates the text because we've handled it as though it must yield to our superior understanding of what our people need to hear. In this way we actually *prevent* our congregations from hearing the message of the Evangelists.

Having reheard Matthew's proclamation as a result of reading the text all the way through for the first time in a while, I thought I had better check my impression with some of the scholarship. I spent some time doing that—and was quite thrilled to find so much corroborating material. There's been a significant shift in the interpretation of Matthew since I was in seminary. It's no longer in vogue to speak of it as the "Jewish Gospel" with a Pentateuchal structure. Today, the emphasis seems to be on the *narrative* structure of Matthew—the *entire* structure, including the genealogy, the birth narratives, and the Passion narrative, which, in the five-books-of-the-Pentateuch concept, were entirely overlooked. Now, instead of the "weak" or "undeveloped" Christology that used to be identified with the First Gospel, a high Christology is identified and tied to the opening verses, the concluding verses, and various other points in between. This is what the more literary and canonical developments in biblical studies have done for preachers. If we approach the books of the Bible as whole documents instead of fragmented ones, a powerful pattern appears that can easily be missed by preaching only from fragments, even if we were to do so for many Sundays as the lectionary dictates. I don't mean to suggest that we should preach from a whole book at a time! But if we have the whole book in our minds, we will have a much more *evangelical* (to use that much-maligned word in its proper context) foundation from which to preach a single passage.

Preachers today tend to go against the grain of the Bible, both Old and New Testaments, because we have been conditioned to shift out of the *theo*logical mode into an *anthropo*logical mode, which means setting the world of the Bible aside. Let's look at a couple of examples. I sometimes wonder how the Apostle Peter would feel about being the subject of so many sermons. In fact, I sometimes think he is many preachers' favorite character. Now, to be sure, Peter does come across in the Gospels as a distinct individual, much more so than any of the other disciples. But this very fact has led generations of preachers to spend so much precious time building up the picture of dear, bumbling, oh-so-human Peter that there is nothing left for the Lord Jesus Christ. Take, for example, the story of the transfiguration. Preachers love to point out that Peter can always be counted on to say something obtuse; in this case he says, "Lord, it is good for us to be here; let me make three booths for you and Moses and Elijah." In the typical sermon, this leads into a discussion of how we human beings always want to preserve the mountaintop moments and fail to understand that we need to go back down into the strain and stress of real life. This, in fact, has become the standard transfiguration sermon. I've heard it at least twenty times.

But in Matthew's story of the event, Peter's line is almost a throwaway in the context of the great revelation of the identity of the Son. Mark uses Peter's words to emphasize the "exceedingly great fear" or "terror" (*ekphobos*) that the disciples felt as the theophany took place. Luke's version emphasizes the nature of the event even more, as the disciples "enter the cloud" with fear (*phobeo*) and fall on their faces. Luke chooses a less emphatic word for "fear" or "terror," but on the other hand, he intensifies the power of the theophany by linking the saying of Peter not with a generalized fear of the presence of the divine but directly with the voice of God identifying Jesus as Son and Messiah, after which the disciples fall silent and tell no one what they have seen. Peter, Luke says, spoke *because he did not know what he was saying*; after the voice ceases speaking, the disciples' voices are stilled. They will not possess the voice they need until after the resurrection.

The effect of the transfiguration story is not to teach a generic lesson about coming down off mountaintops. Each of the evangelists in his own way is showing us how the apocalypse—the revelation—of the Lord Jesus Christ stuns the disciples with the "infinite qualitative distinction" between him and them. This is not a spiritual genius who has achieved some sort of higher level of consciousness. This is the only Son of the Father.

Who Do You Say That I Am?

I have heard countless other sermons that seem almost deliberately to miss the point. Take the story of the Gerasene demoniac, for example. Preachers seem to assume that if they tell the story straight from the Bible, the audience is going to start worrying about animal rights. No child hearing the story properly told would ever be so tender-minded. Children know they are supposed to applaud at the end. One of the most memorable sermons I ever heard was preached by the late lamented Lutheran New Testament scholar Don Juel.[3] He titled it, ironically, "What About My Hogs?" in order to make fun of us and our misplaced concerns. He said that if we're thinking about the pigs we're showing how little we understand the world of Jesus, where pigs were forbidden and unclean, fitting instruments for Jesus' exorcism. No good Jew (no good religious person) would be found roaming about among graves, swine, unclean spirits. Like the demoniac himself, Jesus is out of bounds. Our fixation on the hogs prevents us from understanding that the townspeople in the story are shocked not by the loss of the pigs but by Jesus' display of power.

And listen to this: *God's coming means that other powers are driven off.* As Miroslav Volf has emphasized, the Son of God comes into the world, he does not arrive in neutral territory.[4] He arrives in a world that is occupied by the great Enemy of God, who has a host of demonic powers at his command. No one has proven strong enough to overcome this Enemy. The drama of the exorcisms of the Lord Jesus Christ is that Satan has met his Conqueror.

Don Juel said even more in that sermon. He said that *God chooses first. He doesn't respect our right to choose!* We have the idea that all we need is a little more wisdom and nerve to make the right choice. In fact, "making good choices" is one of the slogans of our day. But the story of the Gerasene demoniac does not tell us to make good choices. Not even our imaginations can be trusted. God has to rend the heavens and come down with a commanding Word.

As you can see, I never forgot that sermon. I have never forgotten the theological punch that it delivered. The meaning of the story was revealed. That's what we should remember from sermons. I used to tell a lot of

---

3. This reconstruction of Juel's sermon is entirely from the handwritten notes that I made in my pew. I was never able to extract an actual copy of the sermon from him, although I asked several times. I sent him a copy of my notes after I typed them up and he seemed pleased with them.

4. *Exclusion and Embrace: A Theological Exploration of Identity, Otherness, and Reconciliation* (Nashville: Abingdon, 1996) 293.

stories about my own experiences in my sermons, but I don't do it anymore. People were remembering my stories instead of the biblical stories. What we want to do in our preaching is to point *beyond ourselves* to the presence of the living God.

I'm not trying to suggest that this is easy. Our entire training—for a good many of us, anyway—has tended to turn us away from this way of preaching. We have been deeply influenced, whether we know it or not, by the imperatives we have heard to make the sermon meet people where they are. But if we do that, then we make little room for the cloud-rending Word to speak. And you all know—but your people probably don't—the context for that allusion:

> O that thou wouldst rend the heavens and come down, that the mountains might quake at thy presence—as when fire kindles brushwood and the fire causes water to boil—to make thy name known to thine adversaries, and that the nations might tremble at thy presence! (Isa 64:1)

It is precisely that Power, comrades in the ministry of the divine Word, it is precisely that Power that invades the preaching of the church.

It is up to us to make clear to our people that we serve a living Lord. This may seem obvious, but indeed it is not. The name of Robert Funk has come up here at our conference. He once wrote a blurb for a Jesus book by an NYU professor, saying that the volume declares "a new gospel that breathes fresh life into the Jesus tradition. It may even bring the sage of Nazareth back to life." This is a classic illustration of the insight of Will Willimon, who wrote that these reconstructionists "tend to begin with [the] assumption . . . that Jesus is dead."[5]

If the preacher preaches as though the Lord Jesus Christ is living and active, like the Word described in Hebrews 4:12, the power of the Holy Spirit will inhabit the speaker's words—not because the speaker is eloquent but because, as the Lord himself promises, "He will glorify me, for he will take what is mine and declare it to you" (John 16:14). We need to depend not on homiletical theories and devices, but on the assurance of the Word of God that it will authenticate itself.

May this offering, a sermon from the Gospel of John, be blessed and vitalized by the same living Word of God and the Spirit of Jesus Christ.

---

5. William H. Willimon, *Conversations with Barth on Preaching* (Nashville: Abingdon, 2006) 45. The source of the Funk quotation is an advertisement for a book by James Carse that ran in several publications.

This sermon was originally preached at Christ Church, Greenwich, Connecticut. The version delivered at the Pro Ecclesia conference was cut somewhat. Here is the original version, which was the principal sermon at a three-hour service and was therefore of greater length.

Good Friday 2011

Sermon by Fleming Rutledge

Text: The Passion according to St. John

WE'RE GOING TO REFLECT together on the Passion narrative from the Gospel of John, but first we need to say something about the controversy surrounding the Fourth Evangelist's use of the term "the Jews." In the Middle Ages, when this passage from John was read on Good Friday, congregations sometimes rose up in anger against the Jews in their communities, calling them "Christ-killers." John's Passion narrative has therefore played a lamentable role in the subsequent tragic history of Christians and Jews.

We must therefore try to understand John's use of the term "the Jews." Sometimes he means simply "the religious leaders" of the Jewish community. More often he seems to mean the religious enemies of Jesus during his ministry. He never, *never* means simply "all ethnic Jews." If he had meant that, then Mary and Martha and Peter and all the disciples and Jesus himself would have to be included in the term "the Jews." John's Gospel comes out of a specific context. When it was being put together, the fateful division between Christians and Jews who did not believe in Jesus was in the process of happening. The Fourth Gospel reflects this growing tension. We might wish this was not so, but in any case it is of first importance that we not hear John saying that "the Jews" are uniquely responsible for the death of Christ.

This problem comes up year after year as performances of Johann Sebastian Bach's *St. John Passion* are scheduled and the text causes offense. A careful look at Bach's work, however, shows that over and over, the texts for the choruses indicate that *all true Christian believers* feel remorse for their part in the death of the Lord. In just the same way, many of the hymns and prayers that we use during Holy Week make it clear that we are *all* responsible for the crucifixion that we remember today. "'Twas I, Lord Jesus, I it was denied thee; I crucified thee."[1]

Bach's *St. John Passion* begins with a chorus that gives a sense of the theology of the Fourth Gospel. It is in the form of a prayer that can be our prayer today:

> O Lord, our Master, your glory fills the whole earth!
> Show us by your Passion
> that you, the true eternal Son of God,
> are triumphant
> even in the deepest humiliation [*der grössten Niedrichkeit*].

Deepest humiliation: that's at the heart of the crucifixion. We need to remember that the meaning of Christ's humiliation was not obvious. The early Christians had to uncover the meaning. Who would worship a man who had been stripped, scourged, mocked, and executed as a common criminal? How could a man who was proclaimed as the "true eternal" Son of God be put to death by degrading and inhuman means? We forget that this central fact of our faith was, and still is, deeply strange and profoundly offensive to ordinary religious sensibilities. It was necessary for the early Christians to explain it. Matthew, Mark, Luke, and John each tell the story, but in different ways. John in particular presents the narrative of the trial and execution of Jesus in a manner that is uniquely his. Even in the deepest humiliation the crucified One is the Lord of glory. Today we will think together about what John is telling us about his death.

A major clue is laid out for us in the first chapter of John's Gospel. Not once but twice, John the Baptist says, "Behold the Lamb of God, who takes away the sins of the world" (John 1:29, 36). The symbolism of this was clear to John's readers, but it's not familiar to us. We need to recall that in the Old Testament rituals, lambs were slaughtered as sacrifices to atone for sin. So from the very beginning, we're let in on the secret: the Son of God is to die for the sin of humanity. But there's more. In John's Gospel, Jesus hangs on the cross at midday, the exact time when the Passover lambs are being killed for the feast; so we say in the Lord's Supper, "Christ our Passover

---

1. "Herzliebster Jesu" ("Ah, Holy Jesus"), by Johann Heermann, 1630; trans. Robert Bridges, 1899.

[lamb] is sacrificed for us" (from 1 Cor 5:7). So, we have two meanings: the sacrificial lamb was offered *for sin*; the Passover lamb was eaten on the night of *deliverance from bondage*. John puts both meanings together: Christ is the Lamb of God who delivers us from bondage to sin and death.

Last Sunday was Palm Sunday. The traditional psalm for that day is Psalm 24: "Who is this King of glory? [It is] the Lord strong and mighty, the Lord strong and mighty in battle." The paradox of the passion, according to John, is that even as Jesus is put to death in the most horrible and shameful way, he is the King of glory. At the same time that he becomes the sacrificial lamb who takes away the sin of the world, he is also victorious over death and mighty in battle against the Evil One. Jesus speaks of this three times in John's Gospel: "Now is the judgment of this world; now shall the ruler [*archon*] of this world be cast out" (John 12:31, also 14:30 and 16:11). This is the way he interprets the battle that will take place on the cross. He will overthrow Satan—the ruler of this world—by means of his death.[2]

The dialogue with Pilate is central to John's theological purpose. The question of the identity of the accused man is at stake. Pilate hasn't a clue. He says to him, "Are you the King of the Jews?" Jesus' answer is mysterious: "If my kingship were of this world, my servants would fight, that I might not be handed over . . . but my kingship is not from the world." Pilate is even more confused; he says, "So you are a king, then?" Jesus throws it back at him: "You say that I am a king." He is refusing to debate Pilate on Pilate's terms. Then he says, "For this I was born, and for this I have come into the world, to bear witness to the truth. Every one who is of the truth hears my voice." Pilate asks, "What is truth?" It's a verbal contest. Those who hear Jesus' voice know that the answer to Pilate's question has already been given. It is given by Jesus himself, at the Last Supper, when he says, "*I am* the Way, and the Truth, and the Life" (John 14:6). Truth in person is now standing before Pilate, and Pilate cannot see him. He sees only a perplexing Jew who has been brought to him for judgment.

The members of John's community in the first century understood that this scene was a dramatic enactment of the identity of Jesus. We today are in the same position. Who is this man who is being condemned? Are we hearing the truth about him? Some of you are believers, but many of

2. The New Testament worldview should be better understood by Christians than it presently is. John and Paul, especially, operate on the assumption (widely held in New Testament times) that the world as we know it is in the grip of Sin and Death (personified as Satan). Humanity has no capacity to liberate itself. Deliverance must come from another sphere of power—another world.

you have questions. Who is Jesus? Who was he then, and who is he now? Is he indeed the "true eternal Son of God," the Word of God made flesh, the Lamb who takes away the sin of the world, the King of glory? Or is this just a story about a gifted Jewish teacher whose reputation was inflated after his death by some enthusiastic but possibly deluded preachers and writers?

The celebrated preacher Will Willimon wrote recently that all of the modern attempts to reconstruct some sort of "historical Jesus" "tend to begin with an assumption . . . *that Jesus is dead.*"[3] This assumption will forever prevent us from understanding who it is that hangs on the cross. Every single thing in the New Testament, every syllable written about Jesus of Nazareth, was written with the presupposition that the crucified One is *alive*, raised from death, triumphant over sin and every form of evil. John's narrative is constructed to show that even on the cross, Jesus is already commanding the future. When he says, "I thirst," he is not saying it because he is perishing with thirst, although he is; he says it in order to fulfil the Scriptures. When he says to the beloved disciple, "Behold, your mother," he is not imparting a moral lesson about sons taking care of their mothers; it's about the new family, the new community that Jesus is establishing in his Name by the power of the Holy Spirit. When he says, "It is finished," he doesn't mean "it's over." He means that he has completed his work. Listen to the words of the Lord in John's account of the Last Supper, as he prays to the Father:

> Father, the hour has come; glorify thy Son that the Son may glorify thee, since thou hast given him power . . . to give eternal life to all whom thou hast given him. And this is eternal life, that they know thee the only true God, and Jesus Christ whom thou hast sent. I glorified thee on earth, having accomplished the work which thou gavest me to do; and now, Father, glorify me in thine own presence with the glory which I had with thee before the world was made. (John 17:1–5)

He is the King of glory; but his glory is concealed from Pilate and the crowds in the street. The mob cries out, "We have no King but Caesar." There is a political dimension to the Passion story. To believe that Jesus is Lord is to learn that Caesar is not Lord, and that got the early Christians into a lot of trouble. You may have seen the extraordinary story on the front page of *The New York Times* last week about the sharply increasing persecution of

---

3. William H. Willimon, *Conversations with Karl Barth on Preaching* (Nashville: Abingdon, 2006) 45. Italics in original.

the house churches in China. The churches in China have tried to make a point of being nonpolitical, but that is no longer possible for them. Either they are loyal to the Communist state, with Jesus as a subsidiary, or they confess Jesus as Lord. One pastor has been detained forty-one times, but he says, "I will not leave my church."[4] God is doing something among the Christians in China. We should pray that the American churches will not be so busy enjoying their privileges that we will fail to see the crucified One calling forth the witness of the endangered Chinese churches. They know that Caesar is not Lord.

What does it mean to believe that a crucified man is the Lord of all glory? A movie called *Of Gods and Men* has been playing for several months in New York to rapturous reviews, but it will probably never get to Greenwich, so you'll have to get the DVD. This movie tells the true story of a small Christian monastery in Algeria during the vicious civil war of the 1990s. In October 1993, the most extreme of the armed Islamic groups, the dread GIA,[5] issued a manifesto: "Foreigners are given thirty days to leave [Algeria]. If they do not, they are responsible for their own deaths."

The Trappist monks had taken a vow of stability, meaning that they were committed to their monastery in the Atlas Mountains for life. They were devoted to their Muslim neighbors, and their devotion was returned; there was a deep bond between the poor local people and their *babas*. The monks offered many services to their neighbors, particularly medical care. If they were to leave, not only would they be violating their vows, but they would be abandoning their friends. The GIA was known for its indiscriminate atrocities, and several nuns and priests had already been killed in the cities. Even though the monks knew they faced the prospect of cruelty and death, they all voted to stay. All of this is depicted faithfully in the movie, but movies are not very good at portraying inner convictions. The story is told much more completely in the book *The Monks of Tibhirine*.[6] The

---

4. Andrew Jacob, "Illicit Church, Evicted, Tries to Buck Beijing," *New York Times*, April 7, 2011, http://www.nytimes.com/2011/04/18/world/asia/18beijing.html?pagewanted=all.

5. *Groupe Islamique Armé*.

6. John W. Kiser, *The Monks of Tibhirine: Faith, Love, and Terror in Algeria* (New York: St. Martin's, 2002). This superb book—highly recommended—gives a thorough portrait of the monks' mental and spiritual struggles, as well as a very useful recent history of Algeria. It also offers hope for Christian witness among Muslims. Robert Wilken was kind enough to send me his review of this book, which is largely laudatory but quite rightly criticizes it for doctrinal mushiness!

monks stayed in their monastery, singing the offices around the clock and serving the people, because of their Christian convictions. They were consciously taking up the cross, as their Lord had bidden them.

In the middle of the night, the armed men came. They entered the unprotected monastery and took the monks away. No one ever saw them alive again. Two months later, their severed heads were found.[7]

But this is not a story of death. This is a story of life. The monks' sacrifice became known throughout Algeria, riven for decades by struggle and bloodshed. The prior, Christian de Chergé, knowing that he might die, had written a testament that was published in the papers. He spoke of love and forgiveness. It was a turning point in a country that had been "drunk on violence."[8] Today the monks are revered as saints throughout Algeria.

You are here today seeking the meaning of the cross. The decisions we face here in Greenwich are not likely to be so dramatic as those in China or Algeria, but there is no Christian anywhere who does not have opportunities to take a more costly path in the name of Christ. It is sin that prevents us from making such choices, but the Lamb of God has conquered sin. It is fear that prevents us from making a courageous witness, but the Lord of glory has delivered us from bondage to fear. To know the Lord of glory is to find the Way, and to know the Truth, and to obtain Life:

> Father, the hour has come; glorify your Son . . . since you have given him power . . . to give eternal life to all whom you have given him. And this is eternal life, that they know thee the only true God, and Jesus Christ whom thou hast sent. *Amen.*

---

7. The exact circumstances of their deaths have never been determined. Weeks after the monks were detained, a tape recording of their living voices was made and delivered to the authorities. Their bodies were never found. Some have theorized that the government executed them and cut off their heads in order to blame the whole thing on the GIA. This is only a theory and has not found wide acceptance.

8. Kiser, *Monks of Tibhirine*, 258.

7

Behold the Lamb of God Who Does *What*?

Gossiping about Jesus and Giving Our Neighbors the (Boney) Finger

Daniel M. Bell, Jr.

"Who do you say that I am?" Perhaps we cannot help endowing this question with great weight because it stands in the Gospel narratives as a kind of watershed moment, when the disciples, specifically Peter, finally (if only temporarily) get the identity of Jesus right. But the truth of the matter is that the question is quite ordinary. In different forms, we raise it all the time. The self-referential form—"Who am I?"—has anchored the modern existential quest for identity and meaning that has driven many a sermon and much of modern theology. In a form closer to the scriptural example, the question is perhaps even more culturally ubiquitous. After all, we spend a great deal of time and energy attending to "What are others saying about me?" and we devote a significant amount of our interpersonal and financial resources attempting to influence the answer to that question. All of which is to say that gossip, attending to what is being said about oneself and others, is an ordinary, significant, and entrenched cultural practice.

So, the earthy truth of this question is that Jesus is engaged in the age-old habit of gossip. But of course, when the object of the gossip is Jesus Christ, the query necessarily exceeds the ordinary concern for human reputation, for this is no mere human who may be seen, known, and interpreted like other persons. Jesus is not like all other persons in the sense that, as Karl Barth observes, Jesus does not exist apart from the grace of His origin, and therefore in virtue of the fact that He is the Son of God.[1]

This is to say, as an inquiry into the reputation of the Son of God, this is not merely gossip about this particular human, Jesus of Nazareth. Rather it is a question about the character and nature of the Gospel, the good news. By virtue of the grace of Jesus' identity as the Son of God, the question of his reputation must necessarily be an inquiry into his relation to God. More specifically, it must be an inquiry into the relationship between this particular one, Jesus, and God's mighty acts of salvation. To ask who Jesus is, is to ask what God is doing to address the human predicament. Thus it is an inquiry into nothing less than the reputation of God. It is gossip taken to the extreme: gossip about God.

Yet, the Gospel context of this question makes it clear as well that gossip reveals as much about the subject of the question as its object. That some say Jesus is John the Baptist, Elijah, or one of the prophets reveals as much, if not more, about the hopes and expectations of those gossiping as it does about the identity of Jesus. This is a phenomenon perhaps most famously noted in relation to the various quests for the historical Jesus, where it has been observed that scholars have peered down the long well of history trying to discern Jesus only to spy their own reflection.

What one says about Jesus discloses much about how one understands the human predicament, who God is and what God is or is not doing to address that predicament. It reveals, to echo the title of J. B. Phillips' famous work, the size of one's God.[2] It reveals what kind of news one believes the good news to be.

But there is yet more to this gossip than self-disclosure. The point is not simply a test of whether one really "gets" who Jesus is or not, as though salvation hinged upon passing a theology exam. The question put to the disciples is not what do you *think* about Jesus but what do you *say* about Jesus. This is to say, this question about gossip is a query of evangelism: Who are you telling *others* that I am?

1. Barth, *Church Dogmatics* IV.2, 91.
2. Phillips, *Your God Is Too Small* (London: Epworth, 1952).

Who Do You Say That I Am?

What follows is an inquiry into Christian gossip about Jesus. What are we telling others about Jesus? Unlike the well-known quests for the historical Jesus, however, I am not so much interested in the historical as the contemporary Jesus. This is to say, the focus here is on several dominant strands of contemporary Christian gossip about Jesus. First, I consider what contemporary Christian gossip about Jesus conveys about God, the human predicament, and what God is or is not doing to address that predicament. Second, I consider what kind of news these contemporary strands of gossip communicate by attending to the results of the National Study of Youth and Religion as presented by Christian Smith and Kenda Creasy Dean. Put bluntly, what can we conclude about the nature of the news spread by this gossip? Is contemporary Christian gossip good news? The study's results are less than encouraging, which brings us to my third move, which suggests a different kind of gossip altogether, namely, that of giving our neighbors the (boney) finger.

I. Gossiping about Jesus

We begin by considering several strands of contemporary Christian gossip about Jesus. Like any good stream of gossip, the contemporary church's gossip about Jesus has many currents and eddies. The four I have chosen are significant for their prominence in mainline North American Christianity but they are by no means comprehensive. Nor are they "pure" in the sense that they do not admit of overlap, mixture, and hybridity. Indeed, there is a certain "family resemblance" between them; they could be viewed as different mutations of a common core, different spectrums of light cast by the sides of a single prism.

The Buddy Jesus

The first strand of contemporary Christian gossip about Jesus can be characterized as the "buddy Jesus," a label borrowed from a popular movie of the recent past. This movie featured a priest disillusioned with the hidebound traditionalism of his church. His faith was revived as his parish developed a campaign ("Catholicism Wow!") to recast the church's image. Central to this revitalization was the replacement of the old "wholly depressing" crucifix in his parish with a statue of the "buddy Christ," of Jesus *sans* cross, winking and smiling while pointing at and giving the viewer a "thumbs up" sign.[3]

Of course, this image was meant as a parody of the faith. However, it comes strikingly close to literal accuracy in portraying one prominent way that Christians talk about Jesus today. We strive to show the world that Jesus is our buddy, that he is relevant, that he fits into our world, satisfies our wants.

Over the course of the last two decades this effort to render Jesus more user-friendly and relevant has taken the form of giving the faith a makeover so that it is more appealing to "seekers" and the "unchurched." The result has been an explosion of "entertainment evangelism"[4] and worship modified to reduce, if not eliminate altogether, that which is strange and off-putting to the uninitiated. Many churches (even professed "evangelical" ones) deliberately no longer talk about sin, suffering, or sacrifice. Confession has fallen by the wayside (or has been abstracted and generalized into oblivion), and the cross is removed or covered up.[5] Congregations are lauded in the denominational presses for such relevant novelties as "tweeting" worship services, transforming sanctuaries into popular movie sets, replacing liturgies with Broadway show tune sing-alongs, holding "drive-in" style services where folks need not get dressed, eat breakfast, or even leave their cars, and celebrating communion in drive-by, self-service style. Likewise, preachers are praised for peppering their sermons with jokes, introducing musical chairs, balloons, funny hats, mime-led communion services, sermons by "Yuk-Yuk the Clown," and updating the eucharistic elements with Diet Coke, cookies, and whipped cream. In this way, it is thought, the church will show Jesus as engaging and satisfying.[6]

Related to this is the strong push for the church to adopt the methods of Madison Avenue and market itself.[7] Thus the centerpiece of a denominational evangelism effort is a multimillion dollar television and radio ad

---

3. *Dogma*, dir. Kevin Smith (Lions Gate, 1999).

4. See Walt Kallestad, *Entertainment Evangelism: Taking the Church Public* (Nashville: Abingdon, 1996).

5. I know of a prominent evangelical congregation that spent $10,000 on a curtain to conceal the cross during its contemporary service.

6. These are all real examples that will remain anonymous because the issue is not particular congregations or denominations but the larger ethos/trends.

7. See Philip Kenneson and James L. Street, *Selling Out the Church: The Dangers of Church Marketing* (Nashville: Abingdon, 1997); George Barna, *Marketing the Church: What They Never Taught You about Church Growth* (Colorado Springs: Navpress, 1988).

campaign designed by a national marketing firm. Judicatories bring in marketing experts to lead workshops on preaching and counseling. Congregations consult specialists to help them segment their local community, identify a niche, and then position themselves to meet the expressed needs of the targeted segment(s). Along these same lines, congregations now advertise themselves as being organized like malls, with programs and ministries described as anchor stores and boutiques.[8] Others market themselves by advertising theater-style seating and cup holders, food courts run by nationally known fast-food chains, and a choice of worship settings.[9]

When the church presents Jesus in this manner, when its gossip says to the world that Jesus is your buddy, what is it saying about God, the human predicament, and the good news? The human predicament seems to be that we lack sufficient service providers.[10] We lack adequate entertainment. Some of our wants are unmet. And the good news is that God can provide and entertain. The church can satisfy those wants.

Jesus the Therapeutic Moralist

Closely related to the talk of Jesus as our buddy is the second strand of gossip, which I identify as "Jesus the therapeutic moralist." The therapeutic moralist Jesus is distinguished from the buddy Jesus by means of his interest in needs instead of wants. Granted, the two can appear indistinguishable because in an advanced consumerist culture it is difficult to separate needs from wants. They can also be indistinguishable insofar as often there is a kind of theological bait-and-switch going on with the buddy Jesus. Jesus is advertised as our buddy, but once we get inside we may be confronted with the therapeutic moralist Jesus, who is not really standing around waiting to entertain and satisfy our wants and whose donuts and coffee come with strings attached in the form of expectations and obligations.

Notwithstanding the way they are often intermingled, whereas the buddy Jesus is one who strives to satisfy the church shoppers'/religious consumers' wants, the therapeutic Jesus is more focused on the modern

---

8. At least one church actually purchased a mall and converted it into the church campus. The worship space is the old Sam's Club.

9. One church I attended actually had a rock climbing wall in the worship space. During the service, although people continuously strolled in and out to get coffee and donuts, I did not see anyone attempt to climb the wall.

10. Barna, *Marketing the Church*, 37.

person's pyscho-spiritual need for interpersonal warmth (with the divine and others) and self-esteem amidst the anomie of (post)modern bureaucratic culture. Furthermore, while this Jesus strives to meet specific needs, he can also be moralistic, imposing obligations on his followers regarding what they need to do to earn their reward and maintain divine approval. This is Jesus not as the ultra-relevant brand or entertainer but as counselor and life coach.

The therapeutic side of this Jesus is perhaps best known, as it has been widely remarked upon. Philip Rieff identified it over forty years ago in his now classic work, *The Triumph of the Therapeutic*.[11] This is the Jesus become therapist for a Gospel reduced to a psychology of self-actualization and self-fulfillment. In its more theological manifestations, this is the Jesus whose primary concern is helping people who were wounded by traditional church recover by feeling good about shedding the confessional, traditional accoutrements of their woundedness. More recently, this Jesus has been tracked by Marsha Witten, whose study of contemporary Protestant preaching reveals a Jesus who aspires to aid us in coping with the anxieties of everyday life by encouraging our growth in self-awareness, relieving our feelings of anxiety and doubt, and providing self-help principles and techniques that will enhance our interpersonal relations and increase our enjoyment of worldly pursuits and goals.[12] This is the Jesus on display in numerous books that purport to offer insights into living and leadership based on Jesus' example.

The moralistic side of this Jesus comes through clearly in the results of the National Study of Youth and Religion, conducted between 2001 and 2008, involving thousands of teenagers and young adults of a variety of denominations and ideological persuasions, across the United States. Time and again the dominant image of the faith that comes through in these interviews is that of Christianity as a set of moral guidelines that one must adhere to if one wishes to prosper here and avoid hell hereafter. As one conservative Protestant teen put it, "If you do the right thing and don't do anything bad, I mean nothing really bad, you know you will go to heaven. If you don't, then you're screwed, that's about it."[13] Christianity is a set of

---

11. Rieff, *The Triumph of the Therapeutic: Uses of Faith after Freud* (New York: Harper & Row, 1966).

12. Witten, *All Is Forgiven: The Secular Message in American Protestantism* (Princeton: Princeton University Press, 1993).

13. Christian Smith with Melinda Lundquist Denton, *Soul Searching: The Religious*

life lessons or principles meant to guide us in making the right decisions and being a good, moral person, which means being nice, kind, pleasant, respectful, responsible, trying to improve, doing one's best to be successful, and so forth.[14]

When the church presents Jesus as a kind of therapeutic moralist, what is it saying about God, the human predicament, and the good news? The human predicament amounts to life in the (post)modern world where the worth of the human personality and warmth of interpersonal relations are under constant threat by the cold impersonality of (post)modern life. But the good news is that we are not alone: Jesus can meet our needs for worth and warmth. He shows that God loves us, and so we can take comfort and consolation in the warmth of one solid interpersonal relationship and the value we have in God's eyes. Furthermore, Jesus provides a plethora of life lessons, moral guidelines, and self-help tips that can help us navigate the stresses of postmodern life.

The Stuffed Jesus

The third form of contemporary Christian gossip about Jesus is what I call the "stuffed Jesus." This is the Jesus who resembles that trophy buck on your eccentric uncle's wall in the sense that this Jesus has been gutted and his meaning and message filled in by a secular ideology, by a way of life that bears no intrinsic connection to the confessions and practices of the faith. The Jesus who is merely a sign, means, or instrument pointing us to the appropriate moral, political, or social option offered by the world (which can be known and practiced apart from Christ or the means of grace). The Jesus who came so that those of us who are perhaps a bit morally challenged or politically obtuse will realize that political liberalism, the family, progressive activism, or a given party's platform, etc., correspond to the way, the truth, and the life.

Unlike the previous two strands of gossip, this Jesus does not have as prominent a public face. There are few Christians who would bluntly state that the Gospel is reducible to a party platform. Although there are some: I know an up-and-coming pastor who as a seminarian once objected to something in class, saying, "I cannot accept this. It goes against my party."

and Spiritual Lives of American Teenagers (Oxford: Oxford University Press) 136.

14. Ibid., 163; Christian Smith with Patricia Snell, *Souls in Transition: The Religious and Spiritual Lives of Emerging Adults* (Oxford: Oxford University Press, 2009) 148–51.

During the 2004 presidential election I came across what appears to be an official campaign poster declaring one pair of candidates "God's Chosen Warriors." And not too long ago in my church someone observed matter-of-factly, "Of course, Democrats don't pray." The point is that for some it seems that Jesus has been gutted and faith and party are synonymous. It is this reality that has given rise to the bumper sticker that reads, "God is not a Republican. Or a Democrat."

Many of us would no doubt reject this rather crude theological taxidermy. But the rather crass stuffing is but the child of more sophisticated thinkers who accepted the modern reduction of Christianity to an apolitical, cultural, spiritual reality and then insisted on Christianity's instrumental value, on its usefulness as the custodian of the values and principles intended to underwrite Western civilization, liberal democracy, human rights, and so forth. I would argue that this remains the dominant ethical paradigm for gossiping about Jesus today on the theological right and left, among Catholics and Protestants. Jesus articulates values that the ethicist, pastor, or layperson then correlates with various concrete secular social and political options.

When the church presents a stuffed Jesus, what is it saying about God, the human predicament, and the good news? The human predicament is not (directly) a matter of unsatisfied consumer wants or unmet human needs. Rather, the problem is the disorder of human life. The human predicament is a matter of the proper ordering of human life, which either has not yet been achieved or is under attack. Furthermore, there are persons who, for whatever reason, fail to recognize the proper order. Therefore, Jesus appears in order to clarify for those of us who do not get it any other way, that we are supposed to be Democrats or Republicans or human rights advocates or family-friendly and so forth.

The Boring Jesus

The last form of contemporary gossip about Jesus I am going to mention is admittedly a bit of a catchall. It gathers up all the sanctimonious trivialities, pious irrelevancies, fudge divinity, and blue ducks that we talk about when we are supposed to be taking about Jesus. Martin Luther King, Jr. denounced the churches of his day for proclaiming pious irrelevancies and sanctimonious trivialities, lofty abstractions signifying nothing. A seminary professor of mine used to denounce "fudge divinity," by which he meant pious rhetoric about God's love that was little more than sugary sentimentality devoid of substance, sort of like candy that tastes good going down but provides little actual nourishment. Luther criticized preachers of his day who would talk about anything, from ancient philosophy to the milk of chickens to blue ducks, rather than talk about the Gospel of Jesus Christ. We might include here the book reviews, movie analyses, and childhood stories that are passed off from the pulpit as preaching the Word.

Such gossip is a telltale sign that the one doing the gossiping has nothing to say. Or rather, such gossipers have nothing to say about Jesus. Apparently, Jesus is just not that interesting, not that exciting, not that compelling, so that after a few years preaching and perhaps a couple of turns through the lectionary cycle, we have nothing left to say about Jesus, so we turn to bland abstractions, sentimentality, and the best-seller's list instead. This is the Jesus who represents that astonishing accomplishment of modern Christianity that Stanley Hauerwas identifies: the boring Jesus. We have somehow managed to make the God of the universe, who moves the sun and the other stars, so innocuous that it is a struggle to maintain our attention, much less the attention of the average teenager or young adult.

When the church gossips about pious irrelevancies and blue ducks, when it all but declares that it has nothing left to say about Jesus, that he is boring in comparison to the latest hit novel or blockbuster movie, what is it saying about God, the human predicament, and what God is doing about that predicament? A single, simple answer is difficult, for sometimes in place of Jesus we are offered sentimental consolation or moralistic self-help for facing modern life or the human condition. Other times we are offered entertainment as the church struggles to justify its existence. In the final analysis, though, the message is that we are alone. And there is no news from on high. Whatever our difficulties and challenges, we must scramble to make do with whatever we can cobble together, be it sentimental escape, Stoic resignation, or self-help in spiritual drag.

2. Are You the One? What Do You See and Hear?

We began with the question Jesus put to others: "Who do you say that I am?" As we move now to consider the outcome of these contemporary strands of gossip about Jesus, we turn to another scene, where the question is put to Jesus. In two of the Gospels, John the Baptist's disciples approach Jesus and ask him, "Are you the one who is to come, or are we to wait for another?"[15] Jesus answers by in effect asking, "What do you see and hear?" And then he recounts that the blind receive their sight, the lame walk, the lepers are cleansed, the deaf hear, the dead are raised, and the poor have the good news preached to them.

What do you see and hear? Historically, this question has been central to Jewish objections to Christianity. You see, the Jews know about the Messiah, and they know what the world is supposed to look like when the Messiah arrives, and the world of Christendom does not exactly meet expectations. In a similar vein, Friedrich Nietzsche, that famous nineteenth-century hater of Christianity, once remarked, "They would have to sing better songs for me to learn to believe in their Redeemer: and his disciples would have to look more redeemed."[16]

I mention these questions regarding what folks see and hear because they nicely situate the results of the National Study of Youth and Religion (NSYR) as reported in the work of Christian Smith and Kenda Creasy Dean.[17] The study and its results are interesting on many levels, especially for a glimpse of the impact or impression that contemporary Christian gossip is making on teens and young adults. What do folks see and hear about Jesus?

NSYR: Indifference

Perhaps the most immediately striking fact revealed by the study is that, contrary to conventional wisdom, American teenagers and youth are not in rebellion against Christianity and the church. While it is true that young adults show a tendency to distance themselves from the particular forms of their parents' religious observance (perhaps loosening ties and attendance with their "home" congregation) as part of their struggle for independence and identity differentiation,[18] as a whole they are not hostile toward religion. To the contrary, both teenagers and young adults report that they are generally positively inclined toward religion and toward the congregations

---

15. Matt 11:2-6; Luke 7:18-23.
16. *Thus Spoke Zarathustra*, part II, "On Priests."
17. Dean, *Almost Christian: What the Faith of Our Teenagers Is Telling the American Church* (Oxford: Oxford University Press, 2010); Smith and Denton, *Soul Searching*; Smith and Snell, *Souls in Transition*.
18. Smith and Snell, *Souls in Transition*, 78, 150.

they know.[19] Nor do they think that the church is full of hypocrites or doubt the integrity of the adults who worship there. Even the tag-line that has become popular in some media and ecclesial circles that youth and young adults are "spiritual but not religious"—that is, turned off by institutionalized religion—is debunked as largely a myth.[20] On the whole, American youth are content and conventional. As Smith observes, countering the commonplace notion that youth are restless, rebellious, and alienated from religion:

> [T]hat impression is fundamentally wrong. What we learned by interviewing hundreds of different teenagers all around the country is that the vast majority of American teenagers are *exceedingly conventional* in their religious identity and practices. Very few are restless, alienated, or rebellious; rather, the majority of U.S. teenagers seem basically content to follow the faith of their families with little questioning. When it comes to religion, they are quite happy to go along and get along.[21]

At first glance, this seems to be good news and perhaps something of a relief to those who are fretting over what to do (and where to get the funds) to change their congregational life so that they are more appealing to what was assumed to be an alienated and antagonistic younger generation. But as Smith and Dean continue with their analysis, cause for relief quickly disappears as it becomes clear that the operative word for the relation of youth to religion is "indifference."[22] As Kenda Creasy Dean writes, "The bad news is the *reason* teenagers are not hostile toward religion: they just do not care about it very much. Religion is not a big deal for them."[23] It functions as a kind of benign, unobtrusive background that evokes little thought or concern. The problem, Smith says, is not youth hostility but "benign 'whateverism.'"[24]

19. Smith and Denton, *Soul Searching*, 61–67.
20. Ibid., 72–82; Smith and Snell, *Souls in Transition*, 251, 295–96.
21. Smith, *Soul Searching*, 119–20.

22. Note that this study did not focus only on liberal, mainline churches. It included Mormons, evangelical white and black churches, Roman Catholics and Jews as well. Hence the results below are not limited to the liberal churches. The study did reveal a difference in levels of commitment between churches. Mormons had the highest percentage of devoted, followed by evangelical white and black churches, followed by mainline Protestantant, then Catholic, then Jewish, then those who identified as nonreligious.

23. Dean, *Almost Christian*, 17.
24. Smith, *Soul Searching*, 266.

When Gossip Goes Bad: Moralistic Therapeutic Deism

It would be thoroughly unsurprising if our first response to this revelation was to lament the failure of youths to embrace the faith that is proffered to them by the church. Or perhaps in a more charitable vein, we might acknowledge our failure to teach and communicate the faith well. But either of these responses would reflect a failure to grasp the lesson of the NSYR. Recall that the study reveals youths to be utterly conventional. By and large, they are *not* rejecting what the church teaches. To the contrary, they are following in the footsteps of their elders, especially their parents.

In other words, the indifference of youths is not the result of a failure to listen or a failure to teach. Rather, it is indicative of the *success* of contemporary Christian gossip. As Dean puts it in a passage worth quoting at length,

> Overall, the challenge posed to the church by the teenagers in the National Study of Youth and Religion is as much *theological* as methodological: the hot lava core of Christianity—the story of God's courtship with us through Jesus Christ, of God's suffering love through salvation history and especially through Christ's death and resurrection, and of God's continued involvement in the world through the Holy Spirit—has been muted in many congregations, replaced by an ecclesial complacency that convinces youth and parents alike that not much is at stake. . . . The problem does not seem to be that churches are teaching young people badly, but that we are doing an exceedingly good job of teaching youth what we really believe: namely, that Christianity is not a big deal, that God requires little, and the church is a helpful social institution filled with nice people focused primarily on "folks like us"—which, of course, begs the question of whether we are really the church at all.[25]

Dean's remark about "whether we are really the church at all" is a reference to what Smith identifies as the message of North American Christianity: Moralistic Therapeutic Deism. There are five tenets of this faith:

1. A god exists who created the world and watches over it.
2. God wants people to be good, nice, and fair to each other, as is taught by the Bible, most world religions, and by our intuitions.
3. The central goal of life is to be happy and feel good about oneself.

---

25. Dean, *Almost Christian*, 11–12.

4. God is not involved in my life except when I need God to resolve a problem.

5. Good people go to heaven when they die.[26]

Much could be said about this theologically. For my purposes, I wish to highlight that it clearly reflects the instrumental character of contemporary Christian gossip, which in its various forms presents Jesus as serving our wants and needs instead of radically changing our lives (including our wants and needs) so that they conform to the holiness of God, so that they are marked by the love and obedience of God. Much contemporary North American Christian gossip seems to be saying that Jesus is determined to see that *our* will be done.

Which, in turn, naturally gives rise to indifference. After all, once the church concedes that the individual's needs or wants are sovereign, once it concedes that Jesus is our buddy, therapist, or life coach, then Christ and the church are important only to the extent that they are able to serve those needs and wants.

And this means that the church makes no difference. What it offers is not good news. What it offers is not really news at all. Rather, it is just more of the same. What we say about Jesus suggests that we are just another service provider, entertainer, (remedial) morals instructor, cheap therapist, poor person's country club, and so forth. We are just another competitor, another brand, on the market of meaning, interpersonal warmth, life lessons, etc.

In the end, much contemporary Christian gossip about Jesus fails to offer the world good news. What it offers is, for the most part, not *repellant*, but neither is it compelling or inviting. Said differently, as the NSYR suggests, this god is too small to hold our attention, to inspire commitment, to drive action or instill purpose and direction. In short, this is a rather benign god who neither calls nor offers much.

3. Good Gossip: Behold the Lamb of God, Who Takes Away the Sin of the World

Such gossip about Jesus hardly sounds like it could give rise to the objection, "These people have been turning the world upside down" (cf. Acts 17:6). Indeed, it is hard to imagine anyone crucifying the object of such

---

26. Ibid., 14. Slightly altered based on Smith's work.

gossip. Indifference seems about right. After all, all the coffee and donuts, clown communions, theater seating, fudge divinity, pious irrelevancies, and life lessons in the world are not going to make such gossip *more* attractive than the golf course, the coffee bar, the latest self-help best seller, or Seventh-Day Horizontalism (i.e., just sleeping in).[27]

What Is the Gospel?

Which returns us to where we began, with Jesus' query to the disciples: "Who do you say that I am?" What is good gossip about Jesus? What is the good news that we should be telling others about Jesus?

Admittedly, at first glance this might seem to be a rather simplistic and all-too-basic question to raise. Certainly, if one considers the ways the mainline churches (and congregations) approach the problems of indifference and decline exposed by the NSYR, one would think this question out of place, for it is never raised. Instead it is taken for granted that we all know the good news and the problem is simply a matter of communication. So we brainstorm new programs and ministries, new PR campaigns and slogans, new organizational structures and mission emphases. Always on the assumption that we know the good news.

But the NSYR suggests that we do not. It suggests that we do not know the Gospel. And this holds not simply for the least committed fringe of the church or particular congregation. After all, if that were all that the study revealed, then it would be thoroughly unremarkable. Every pastor and congregational leader knows—as does every professor—that only a handful in any group or class really "get it." Nor does it hold for only one end of the ideological spectrum—although there are differences in commitment levels reflected between ideological perspectives. Rather, bad gossip is endemic across the whole. The problem is not that only a few "get it" but that the many get it only too well—and what they are getting is not good news. As Dean suggested, the problem is not a failure to communicate but the success of what we are communicating. After all, it is not the fringe of the church that is spreading the various deficient forms of gossip cited earlier but the local and national leadership. Every example I cited comes not from an Internet search for obscure or quirky church practices but from mainline churches and what they lift up and celebrate.

---

27. The phrase "Seventh-Day Horizontalism" is Will D. Campbell's.

Who Do You Say That I Am?

Several years ago, in the process of conducting a search to fill a faculty position at the seminary where I teach, someone came up with the idea of asking every candidate in the course of an interview to summarize the Gospel. At first I thought it a juvenile question, but then I was stunned and saddened by some of the responses I heard from persons deeply implicated in teaching the faith and leading the church. And for several years now, as I have served on boards and panels interviewing new pastors as well as candidates for church leadership in two mainline denominations, I have been struck by the pervasive inarticulateness, superficiality, or downright vacuousness of the gossip coming from so many of these future leaders. Although it is anecdotal and humbling for one involved in forming such leaders, it certainly comports with the findings of the NSYR.

What is the Gospel? What should we tell the watching and listening world about Jesus? Who do we say Jesus is? The good news is not that God provides us with entertainment or satisfaction of our spiritual wants. The good news is not that Jesus provides us with company, consolation, advice for attaining success in our interpersonal relations and self-selected life goals, or motivation as a party foot soldier, culture warrior, or social activist.

The good news, which the early church never tired of announcing to the world, is that God became human that humanity might become divine. The good news is that God has drawn near to us so that we might become something better.

In this regard I find John 1:29 to be a particularly apt starting point for thinking about what good gossip about Jesus looks like today. There John the Baptist declares, "Behold the Lamb of God, who takes away the sin of the world." Is this not the starting point for Christian gossip? For everything Christianity says about Jesus? About who he is and what he does, about what the human predicament is and what God is doing to address it through this particular Jew?

This is news that exceeds the inevitably empty promise of satisfying our consumer wants. This is news that surpasses therapy and consolation for easing the anxieties and stresses of our (post)modern lives. It is more than the wise words of a motivational speaker, self-help guru, moral master, or party whip.

"Behold the Lamb of God" is good news because Christ offers not a better version of an old life, but new life. "So if anyone is in Christ, there is a new creation" (2 Cor 5:17). Christ does not aspire to help us cope with the challenges and stresses of the old, passing age, but to live now according to the new age, in righteousness and holiness, which God prepared beforehand to be our way of life (Eph 2:10). Christ does not come to help us pick and choose among the politics of this age, but so that "through the church the wisdom of God in its rich variety might now be made known to the rulers and authorities" (Eph 3:10).

Behold the Lamb of God, who takes away the sin of the world. We are fallen and we cannot get up. We are stuck in the muck and mire of sin. And it is killing us. As Genesis 3 makes clear, it sets us against God, one another, and the rest of creation. Sin is destroying our selves, our families, our neighborhoods and communities, and the wider world.

But the good news is that God in Christ takes away the sin of the world. The good news is that in Christ the civil war that is sin has come to an end. The news that is really news is that Christ does not just help us cope with sin; he takes it away. He does not just bear sin; he bears it away. He does not just deal with the guilt of sin; he breaks the power of sin. He does not simply justify; he also sanctifies.

Freedom from sin in Christ: This is the good news. This is good gossip about God.

Giving Our Neighbors the Finger: Reflecting the Difference Christ Makes

Matthias Grünewald's famous painting *Crucifixion* captures this well. In the painting, John the Baptist points a boney finger at the Christ on the cross, a visual presentation of John 1:29. This is what good gossip about Jesus is all about. Good gossip about Jesus is a matter of giving our neighbors the finger. It is about our lives—individually and corporately—functioning as a boney finger pointing to the Lamb of God who takes away the sin of the world. Put a little differently, good gossip is about our lives reflecting the difference that Christ makes in the world, the name of that difference being, of course, salvation.

In this regard, on occasion I will put a question to seminarians. It is, however, a question that can and should be put to all of us, lay or ordained, novices or those stooped in service. In fact, it could be viewed as a kind of midrash on Mark 8:29: How (or even would) our lives and churches change if it were irrefutably proven tomorrow that the whole Jesus thing was a hoax? If an archeologist stumbled across Jesus' body in a grave, revealing him to be just another in a long line of messianic dreamers?

If the church's job is to entertain, satisfy consumer wants, offer cheap therapy and remedial moral guidance, or serve as a recruiting station for secular politics and causes, then whether Jesus is alive or dead would not matter really. Whether Jesus is dead or not would not fundamentally alter our gossip about meeting needs, satisfying wants, and so forth. After all, that is pretty much what we are doing now, and as the young persons interviewed in the NSYR suggest, Jesus makes no difference.

Good gossip, on the other hand, reflects the difference Christ makes in the world. It enables the unchurched to see what the Lamb is doing here and now in the world through the church. Good gossip is a matter of the church functioning as a city on the hill, whose light prompts those in the darkness of sin to turn and receive the Lamb (Matt 5:16).

Good gossip is a matter of living in such a way that if Jesus were just a deluded dreamer, then our lives should make no sense at all. The difference we reflect—like loving our enemies and praying for them, speaking the truth in love, forgiving not just seven times but seventy times seven, giving all that we have in service to our neighbors, especially the poor, being chaste in singleness and marriage—should make absolutely no sense at all. Where is the entertainment or market value in such practices?

Good gossip is a matter of living as an answer to Nietzsche and his ilk: Living as evidence, icons—"living letters," as Paul would have it—that Jesus really does take away the sin of the world. After all, how will the world know that redemption is possible if it does not see a redeemed people? How will the world know that Jesus is indeed the Lamb of God who takes away the sin of the world if it does not see a holy people, a people being set free from sin? How will the world know that it can be redeemed from its hatreds, violence, lust, greed, and envy if it does not see an alternative way of life? How will it know that it is not trapped in the civil war of sin if it does not see a people sharing Christ's peace, crossing divisions and seeking reconciliation?

Good gossip about Jesus is a matter of living holy, virtuous lives in all that we do—as families, friends and neighbors, coworkers, public servants—lives that cause others to perk up and take notice: Jesus did that to you? Tell me more. Let me into that funny hot tub (the font) and pass those *hors d'oeuvres* (bread and wine).

A Contradiction Full of Promise

At this point a potential misunderstanding of the claim that good gossip entails reflecting the difference Christ makes in the world needs to be addressed. This is the specter of sectarianism. Does not the rejection of Jesus as buddy, therapist, moral guide, and activist smack of simply withdrawing from the world? Is this a call to court irrelevance?

To be sure, the Lamb of God who takes away the sin of the world is no ultra-cool buddy Jesus. He is strange. He has no form or majesty that we should look at him, nothing in his appearance that we should desire him (Isa 53:2). But strangeness in itself is not a problem. As the NSYR suggests, the real problem with Christian gossip is its complete lack of strangeness, its utter banality, even triviality.

Although it goes against the grain of what currently passes for conventional wisdom, the problem is not strangeness but that the uninitiated are given so little reason to endure our strangeness. In this regard, consider the early church in which catechumens would endure the rigors of a lengthy and perhaps dangerous catechesis without sharing in the mysteries (recall such instruction and participation came after baptism). Here was a strangeness that was interesting, compelling, inviting. It was a strangeness that sparkled with the allure of something greater, something grand, something worth giving one's life to and for, even if you did not know exactly what that was at the outset.

In other words, the point is not to court irrelevance. Good gossip about Jesus does not take pride in being contrarian. Reflecting the difference Christ makes should not be confused with the staunch oppositionalism and sheer antagonism of H. Richard Niebuhr's "Christ against Culture."[28]

Rather, our strangeness is the glimmer, in the words of St. Paul, of "a more excellent way" offered to the world. Barth captures this well when he writes, "[The Church] exists . . . to set up in the world a new sign which is radically dissimilar to [the world's] own manner and which contradicts it in a way which is full of promise."[29]

Our strangeness is not a matter of withdrawal but of evangelism. It is the promise offered to the world of something different, something better for the world. Of peace with God and one another through Christ, who takes away the sin of the world, breaks down the dividing walls of hostility,

---

28. Niebuhr, *Christ and Culture* (New York: Harper, 1951).
29. *Church Dogmatics* IV/3.2, 779.

and reconciles all in love. In a world so obviously and terribly afflicted by sin, what could be more relevant than that?

Along the same lines, giving our neighbors the boney finger is not simply a rejection of enjoyment, satisfaction, meeting needs, companionship and consolation, moral guidance, and social-political activism. After all, as the Westminster Divines remind us, our end is enjoyment of God. And as Augustine reminds us, our hearts find satisfaction in God. And as Aquinas notes, salvation is about companionship/friendship with God, and with one another through God. And as Scripture suggests, salvation has a moral as well as sociopolitical form. We are called to imitate Christ, and we are made citizens and ambassadors of the rule/city/kingdom of God.

But this enjoyment, satisfaction, companionship, consolation, moral guidance, and sociopolitical activism are different from simply meeting the manufactured wants and self-identified needs of the age. It is different from simply supplying troops for the world's social and political divisions. In this way, we can say that bad gossip about Jesus is not simply wrong; rather, it is a parody of good gossip. It is born of the proper evangelistic sensibility that Christ offers what the world wants and needs, but it is insufficiently Christoform in its grasp of what we need and what Christ offers.

As a result, it fails to discern the often paradoxical way in which Christ meets our needs and wants and supplies meaning to our lives. As the means of grace, the disciplines of the Christian life, suggest, we find by losing, receive by giving, enjoy by laboring and serving, live by dying.

Instead of cheap therapy we are given a cross. Instead of meaning, we are enlisted in a journey whose meaning we may not entirely discern until the race is over. Instead of shoring up our sovereign selves, we are decentered in service to our neighbors. Instead of a browbeating moralism, we are empowered to do the impossible (love, forgive, serve, die, rise . . .)! Instead of picking sides amidst the politics of division, clashing wills and competing ends, we have been given a ministry of reconciliation for the renewal of communion in the common good, a eucharistic politics, which does not preclude our working with all persons of good will, but cannot be reduced to any secular vision.

Conclusion

Whereas scholars involved in the quest for the historical Jesus are generally criticized for mistaking their own reflection for Jesus, good gossip about

Jesus must be a reflection of Christ's body, the church.[30] This is to say, there ought to be a certain isomorphy between Jesus and Christians such that when folks look for Jesus they should see him in the life of the church. The best gossip is that of our lives as they reflect the difference Christ makes in the world, as they point to the Lamb of God, who really does take away the sin of the world.

Who do we say that Jesus is? Dare we give our neighbors the boney finger? Dare we post on our church marquees—and display in our lives—"Freedom from sin available here, in Christ"?

---

30. See James 1:22–25.